The Sitwells:
Edith, Osbert, and Sacheverell

Twayne's English Authors Series

Kinley E. Roby, Editor

Northeastern University

TEAS 457

THE SITWELLS: SACHEVERELL, EDITH, AND OSBERT
Cecil Beaton photograph courtesy of Sotheby's London.

The Sitwells:
Edith, Osbert, and Sacheverell

By G. A. Cevasco

St. John's University

Twayne Publishers
A Division of G. K. Hall & Co. • *Boston*

The Sitwells: Edith, Osbert, and Sacheverell
G. A. Cevasco

Copyright © 1987 by G. K. Hall & Co.
All rights reserved.
Published by Twayne Publishers
A Division of G. K. Hall & Co.
70 Lincoln Street
Boston, Massachusetts 02111

Copyediting supervised by Lewis DeSimone
Book production by Janet Zietowski
Book design by Barbara Anderson

Typeset in 11 pt. Garamond
by Modern Graphics, Inc., Weymouth, Massachusetts

Printed on permanent/durable acid-free paper
and bound in the United States of America

Library of Congress Cataloging-in-Publication Data

Cevasco, G. A. (George A.)
  The Sitwells : Edith, Osbert, and Sacheverell.

  (Twayne's English authors series ; TEAS 457)
  Bibliography: p.
  Includes index.
  1. Sitwell, Edith, Dame, 1887–1964—Criticism and
interpretation.   2. Sitwell, Osbert, 1892–1969—Criticism and
interpretation.   3. Sitwell, Sacheverell, 1897–   —Criticism and
interpretation.   4. English literature—20th century—History and criticism.
I. Title.   II. Series.
PR6037.I8Z575   1987   820'.9'00912   87–12136
ISBN   0–8057–6953–6 (alk. paper)

To the memory of my mother,
Anna Cevasco
10 January 1893–29 April 1986

Contents

About the Author

G. A. Cevasco, an associate professor of English at St. John's University, New York, completed his undergraduate study at St. John's and his graduate study at Columbia University. A Fellow of the Royal Society of Arts, his publications include ten books and monographs, dozens of scholarly articles, and over three hundred book reviews. Most of his work has appeared in American journals, but he has also been published in England, Ireland, Canada, Italy, France, Taiwan, and the Philippines. His previous book in Twayne's English Authors Series is a bio-critical study of the nineties poet John Gray, a prominent member of the Oscar Wilde circle remembered especially for his *Silverpoints*.

Preface

Edith, Osbert, and Sacheverell Sitwell delighted in their creativity, their compulsion to be different, and their individual contributions to contemporary literature. Filled with ambition and a sense of loyalty to one another, the trio shared similar views on art and eagerly encouraged one another to greater achievement.

Early in the 1920s, they emerged as a literary cult of three, giving every appearance of being by themselves a self-contained artistic movement. To speak of the Sitwells as a collective entity was then a commonplace. Were they not—for good or ill—proponents of their own modern movement, a curious amalgam of cubism, futurism, and dadaism? The Sitwells, it soon became obvious, were not ordinary writers. They determined to become unquestioned luminaries of literature—and they achieved their goal. A considered estimate of their individual accomplishments is overdue.

Their lives have been covered in sufficient detail in several recent biographies, and each of the trio wrote an autobiography. In Osbert's case, his autobiography runs to five volumes. Why, then, another book on the Sitwells? The answer is simple: not one of the studies already written about the Sitwells comes close to what this present volume attempts.

Edith, the eldest of the trio, was the most prominent. When she died on 9 December 1964, hundreds of leading newspapers throughout the world carried the sad news. The *New York Times,* for one, gave a good indication of her importance in modern literature by featuring her obituary on its first page and continuing for seven or eight more columns, complete with photographs, on another page.[1] Most of the important things that should have been noted were, but the *New York Times* made no mention of the view that had John Masefield (who died in 1967) predeceased Edith, she might have been declared his successor as England's poet laureate.

Those who prefer to argue against such a contention claim she would not have been the recipient of such a distinction because (1) she was too eccentric; (2) she was a woman, and no woman had ever been poet laureate of England; and (3) she was a convert to the Roman Catholic church. Each of the three negative reasons for possibly not granting her the laureateship makes her an even more interesting individual to read about; and, on the positive side, there is of course the brilliance of her poetry, literary criticism, social history, and fiction.

"Though many notable literary figures . . . have testified to the importance of Dame Edith's poetry, there has been little careful reading of her poems," one critic has complained. "We have been too much in the habit of dismissing her as the interesting, but . . . eccentric stylist of *Facade.*" What is really needed, this same critic maintains, are not additional biographical studies but "further assessment of her *Collected Poems* as a canon or work . . . and a close study of the more substantial of her individual poems and prose works."[2] This volume aims to do just that.

To write of Edith and ignore her brothers, however, is to ignore the full story. Not only were Osbert and Sacheverell equally important figures in their own right but to trace the closeness and the influence of one Sitwell on another is a prerequisite to proper evaluation of their work; and yet it is important to distinguish carefully among them. They were not a family menagerie, as their adverse critics often charged, though, as Sacheverell once observed, "if you are two brothers and a sister and you all write poetry, it is extremely hard not to be lumped together as a group."[3]

"Osbert, Sacheverell and I are extremely displeased when we are treated as if our works are a mass production," Edith likewise complained. "We do not like to be treated as if we were an aggregate Indian god, with three sets of legs and arms, but otherwise indivisible."[4] Although this volume considers all three of the Sitwells, it focuses on the works of each as unique and special. For only early in their careers did they collaborate; later they followed their own aesthetic inclinations and wrote in their own individualistic fashion. Indeed, they wrote so much that to write of them in a single volume is Sisyphean in its implications. No attempt, accordingly, has been made to be critically all-inclusive, though virtually all of their works are considered, mainly to indicate how and why one work led to another. Only those judged the most significant are discussed in detail.

The introductory chapter is biographical, taking the Sitwells principally from their earliest years up to the launching of their careers. Beyond the first chapter, biography plays at best a supportive role; for thereafter the focus is analytical and critical. The second chapter, for example, deals with their earliest poetry and the founding and editing of their own periodical, *Wheels.* The following chapter considers their collaboration on *Facade,* which made Edith's reputation but left Osbert and Sacheverell still to make theirs. Succeeding chapters then cover the chief works of each in chronological order. A final chapter evaluates the Sitwells collectively and individually and assesses their contribution to contemporary literature.

The extent of my indebtedness to biographers and critics of the Sitwells can be read from my notes and bibliography. I must also specifically thank Cathy Henderson, research librarian at the Humanities Research Center at the University of Texas, Austin, for obtaining permission for me to examine its extensive Sitwell Collection. The Sitwell Family Archives at the Humanities Research Center, a trove of primary source material, contains hundreds of their notebooks and journals, thousands of letters, dozens of photographs and portraits, and practically all the manuscripts of Osbert and Sacheverell and a high percentage of Edith's.

Additionally, I must thank Sacheverell Sitwell, who was kind enough to respond to questioning letters. Finally, I am most appreciative of a research leave granted me by St. John's University; without the time the leave allowed me, I would not have been able to initiate my research or complete this study of the Sitwells—the first to focus on their works and assess their reputations.

G. A. Cevasco

St. John's University

Chronology

1887   Edith Sitwell born 7 September.

1892   Osbert Sitwell born 6 December.

1897   Sacheverell Sitwell born on 15 November.

1915   Edith's *The Mother and Other Poems*, a booklet of verse.

1916   First cycle of *Wheels*, the Sitwell's own periodical. *Twentieth Century Harlequinade and Other Poems*, a collection of Edith's and Osbert's verse.

1917   *Wheels*, second cycle.

1918   *Wheels*, third cycle. Edith's *Clowns' Houses*, verse; Sacheverell's *The People's Palace*, verse.

1919   *Wheels*, fourth cycle. Osbert and Sacheverell mount a controversial exhibition of avant-garde art at London's Mansard Gallery. Osbert's first verse collection, *Argonaut and Juggernaut*.

1920   *Wheels*, fifth cycle. Edith's *The Wooden Pegasus*, verse.

1921   *Wheels*, sixth cycle. Osbert's *At the House of Mrs. Kinfoot*, a satirical poem.

1922   Sacheverell's *The Hundred and One Harlequins*, verse.

1923   Public recitation of *Facade* at London's Aeolian Hall on 12 June. Edith's *Bucolic Comedies*, verse; Osbert's *Out of the Flame*, verse.

1924   Edith's *The Sleeping Beauty*, her most ambitious poem to date; Osbert's first fiction collection; Sacheverell's *Southern Baroque Art*, first prose work, and *The Thirteenth Caesar*, verse.

1925   Sacheverell marries Georgia Doble. Edith's *Troy Park*, poetry collection; Osbert's *Discursions on Travel, Art and Life*, volume of essays.

1926   Edith's *Elegy on Dead Fashion*, a poem; Osbert's first novel, *Before the Bombardment*; Sacheverell's *All Summer in a Day*, an autobiographical fantasia.

1927   Osbert and Sacheverell's *All at Sea,* a play, has three-night run at London's Arts Theatre Club. Edith's *Rustic Elegies,* verse; Osbert's *England Reclaimed,* poetry; Sacheverell's *German Baroque Art* and *Cyder Feast,* poetry.

1929   Edith's major poem, *Gold Coast Customs;* Osbert's second novel, *The Man Who Lost Himself;* Sacheverell's *Gothick North.*

1930   Edith's *Collected Poems* and *Alexander Pope,* a biographical study.

1931   Sacheverell's *Spanish Baroque Art.*

1932   Edith's *Bath,* a volume of social history; Sacheverell's *Mozart.*

1933   Royal Society of Literature awards Edith its medal and membership; she publishes a prose study, *English Eccentrics;* Osbert's novel, *Miracle on Sinai;* Sacheverell's *Canons of Giant Art,* poetry.

1934   Osbert succeeds father as baronet. Edith's *Aspects of Modern Poetry;* Sacheverell's *Liszt.*

1935   *Penny Foolish,* Osbert's essays; Sacheverell's *Scarlatti.*

1936   Edith's biography, *Victoria of England;* Sacheverell's *Collected Poems,* two cultural studies, *Conversation Pieces* and *Narrative Paintings,* and autobiography, *Dance of the Quick and the Dead.*

1937   Edith's *I Live under a Black Sun,* first novel.

1938   Edith, Osbert, and Sacheverell deliver a series of lectures on "Aspects of National Genius" at London University. Osbert's *Those Were the Days,* fourth novel.

1939   *Escape with Me! An Oriental Sketch Book,* essays on Osbert's travels through the Far East.

1940   Edith's *Edith Sitwell's Anthology* and *Poems Old and New,* anthologies; Sacheverell's *Mauretania,* journal of trip to North Africa, and *Sacred and Profane Love,* essays on art and artists.

1941   Edith's *Look! The Sun,* anthology; Osbert's *A Place of One's Own,* novel, and short-story collection, *Open the Door.*

1942   Edith's *Street Songs.*

1943   Osbert's *Selected Poems;* Sacheverell's *Splendours and Miseries,* cultural essays.

1944   Edith's *Green Songs and Other Poems;* Osbert's *Sing High! Sing Low!,* essays.

1945   Edith's *The Song of the Cold,* poetry; Osbert's autobiography, *Left Hand, Right Hand;* Sacheverell's *British Architects and Craftsmen.*

1946   Edith's *Fanfare for Elizabeth,* biography; Osbert's autobiography, *The Scarlet Tree.* St. Andrews University awards Osbert an honorary doctorate of laws.

1947   Leeds University confers an honorary doctorate upon Edith.

1948   Edith and Osbert visit the United States; lecture and read their poetry. *Facade* performed at New York's Museum of Modern Art; enthusiastically received. Osbert's *Great Morning,* third autobiographical volume; Sacheverell's *The Netherlands.*

1949   Edith's *Canticle of the Rose,* poem. American Institute of Arts and Letters names her an Honorary Associate and Durham University confers an honorary doctorate. Osbert's fourth autobiographical volume, *Laughter in the Next Room.*

1950   Edith and Osbert visit Hollywood; entertained by its producers and stars. Osbert declared an Honorary Associate of the American Institute of Arts and Letters; completes fifth volume of autobiography, *Noble Essences: A Book of Characters.* Sacheverell publishes a journal, *Spain.*

1951   Oxford University confers an honorary doctorate on Edith. Sheffield University awards Osbert an honorary doctorate of laws. Sacheverell embarks upon a one-man lecture tour of the United States.

1953   Edith's *Gardeners and Astronomers,* poetry; Osbert's *Collected Stories.*

1954   Edith named a Dame Commander of the Order of the British Empire; her *Collected Poems* and Sacheverell's *Portugal and Maderia.*

1955   Edith converts to Roman Catholicism. Sheffield University confers an honorary degree on Edith.   •

1956   Osbert named a Commander of the British Empire. Sacheverell's *Denmark.*

1957   Sacheverell's *Arabesque and Honeycomb,* travel guide to the Middle East.

1958   Edith's *Atlantic Book of British and American Poetry,* anthology of verse. Osbert elevated to Companion of Honour of the British Empire.

1959   Sacheverell, after travels through Japan, completes *Bridge of the Brocard Sash,* and autobiographical volume, *Journey to the Ends of Time.*

1961   Sacheverell's *Golden Wall and Mirador,* observations on Peru.

1962   A celebration concert in honor of Edith's seventy-fifth birthday held at London's Royal Festival Hall; *pièce de résistance:* recitation of *Facade.* Edith's *The Outcasts,* her last volume of poetry, and *The Queens and the Hive,* a biography of Elizabeth of England and Mary of Scotland; Osbert's *Tales My Father Taught Me,* a postscript to his autobiographical sequence.

1963   Osbert completes his last book, *Pound Wise,* a collection of essays.

1964   Elizabeth dies on 9 December.

1965   Posthumous publication of Edith's last book, *Taken Care Of,* her autobiography.

1969   Osbert dies on 4 May. Sacheverell succeeds to the baronetcy.

1972   Sacheverell's *For Want of a Golden City,* autobiographical volume.

1982   Sacheverell's sixteenth volume of poetry, *An Indian Summer.*

Chapter One

Family Matters

Recollections and Relations

On a summer morning in 1901 Sir George Reresby Sitwell was strolling through his vast gardens at Renishaw Hall, Derbyshire, with his young son Osbert at his side. Though only nine at the time, Osbert never forgot the day. All his life he treasured his recollections of the garden as it looked that morning; its multicolored flowers, the wide expanse of green woodland and bordering lake made an indelible impression upon his mind. Just as memorable as the ground scenery, the dramatic effect of cloud and sun in the sky, were certain words spoken by his father.

Sir George had been droning on about some of his ancestors, how outstanding many of them had been and what they had accomplished. "It's something quite evident . . .," he said, "that we've been working up toward something for a long time, for well over a century."[1] Osbert admits to a slight lift of his heart, although he was not convinced that his father realized the implications of what he had said. More than likely, Sir George was thinking of future Sitwell governors and proconsuls who would be "supreme over the wastes and teeming cities of an empire, shining somewhere among his descendants . . . " (*LH*, 7).

As Sir George made plain to Osbert, members of the Sitwell family, whose name (Cytewel? Citwell? Sitewell?) could be traced back to 1301, were by blood and circumstance extraordinary beings. Sir George knew all this because one of his passions was genealogy. He himself had documented in great detail much of the history of his forebears. The foundation and growth of the Sitwell line was one of his chief interests. He had learned all there was to learn about the family seat at Renishaw and the succession of the baronetcy from Sir Sitwell Sitwell, who was elevated to that rank in 1808.

Most prominent among the Sitwell progenitors, Sir George impressed upon Osbert, were kings of France and the English Plantagenets. Then, too, there were such family dignitaries as Robert

1

Bruce and the Macbeths. One Sitwell after another distinguished himself all through the Middle Ages. During the Elizabethan period, in collateral lines, were the great Lord Chancellor Francis Bacon and Shakespeare's patron Henry Wriothelesey, the third earl of Southhampton. In the seventeenth century, among many other Sitwells, there was the eminent mathematician Dr. John Wallis, custodian of the archives at Oxford University and an original member of the Royal Society. Admiral Boscawen, Flora MacDonald, and the marquess of Granaby were three well-known figures of the eighteenth century who had Sitwell blood in their veins. And in the nineteenth century, Arthur Wellesley, the duke of Wellington, was the great-uncle of Osbert's grandmother.

Young Osbert could not dispute his father: the Sitwells were an illustrious, imperial, influential family. But on the debit side, there were just as many eccentrics as great movers among them. Osbert's great-great-grandfather, Sir Sitwell Sitwell, is a prime example.

A great builder, Sir Sitwell Sitwell added dozens of stables, stalls, and paddocks to Renishaw, but it was the massive gates and triumphal arches that made his architectural escapes seem extreme. During one of his building sprees in 1806, he had a special ballroom constructed specifically for a rout he gave for the prince regent. And among some of the stranger things Sir Sitwell Sitwell is reputed to have done, it is said that in 1810 he purchased a mile of scarlet carpet to spread from his castle to the sea to walk upon whenever he or his guests went for a dip. On the evening of his death, his revenant appeared, so it is claimed, while his body was being waked in the family library; and then several times thereafter.

Sir George on occasion even outdid Sir Sitwell Sitwell. A proper sort of Englishman who always thought of himself as occupying center stage, Sir George would appear in white tie and tails at dinner time regardless of where he might be. One day he decided to beautify his estate by painting blue Chinese characters on his white cows. Possibly his chief claim to fame, or so he believed, was that he captured a spirit at the British National Association of Spiritualists.

Today Sir George is remembered less for his idiosyncratic behavior and his spirit chasing and more—though he would have been reluctant to admit it—for having been the father of three distinguished writers. Never in his wildest dreams, when he dutifully informed Osbert that the Sitwell family had been "working up to something," did Sir George believe it would be the mark Edith, Osbert, and Sacheverell would make in modern literature.

There had been writers in the family before; even he had written essays, monographs, and a volume entitled *An Essay on the Making of Gardens.*[2] Writing to Sir George, however, was at best only an incidental accomplishment, part of the general makeup of a cultured man, hardly an affair to which a serious individual might devote all his energy, time, and talent. One day, in fact, he warned his children about a cousin's friend who killed himself by writing a novel; and when he first heard of Edith's success with poetry, he lamented that she had made "a great mistake by not going in for lawn tennis."[3]

False Expectations

That Edith should dwell upon poetry was a disappointment to Sir George, but Edith claims that she was a disappointment to him and her mother from the day she was born. On 7 September 1887 they were eagerly awaiting their first heir, a son. A female would never do. "My parents were strangers to me from the moment of my birth," Edith later remarked. "I was in disgrace for being a female . . ."[4]

Whether more of the blame for the strained relations Edith experienced with her parents should be placed on her father or her mother, or both, or on her own intractability, there is little doubt that her early years were difficult for all three. More concerned with his own pursuits than with his young daugher, Sir George spent little time with her. Lady Ida, Edith's mother, a victim of lassitude and ennui, spent long hours in bed. Left mainly to the servants, Edith at least received from them a measure of understanding and affection.

Whenever she felt morose or lonely she looked into books, and, having an insatiable curiosity, by the time she was three she had taught herself to read. Hans Christian Andersen's *Fairy Tales* became an early favorite. Some of the tales that she read again and again, it must have seemed, mirrored her own life. Aware that she had not inherited her mother's beauty, she was intrigued in particular by "The Ugly Duckling." Like the swan that was hatched among ducklings and mocked as an ungainly member of the brood, she too, in her childhood fancy, hoped to be properly recognized some day. That neither her father nor her mother had ever dreamed that she might turn into a majestic swan made her an even more difficult child.

Osbert's birth on 6 December 1892 when Edith was five did not improve matters. Osbert was as consciously welcomed into the Sitwell family as Edith had been unconsciously rejected. Inasmuch as she had not felt the love of her parents before Osbert's arrival, his presence in the nursery did not generate an inordinate sibling rivalry. As he himself later noted in his first autobiographical volume, *Left Hand, Right Hand,* Edith always expressed a fondness for him and focused a childish animosity on the real and imagined indifference of Sir George and Lady Ida toward her (*LH,* 41).

Osbert was not only a boy; he was plump, lively, and lovable. Sir George, moreover, considered his first-born son a valuable extension of his own personality. As a consequence, Osbert's earliest years were unusually happy. Few children receive the attention bestowed upon him. He was privileged to have the love of which Edith apparently was deprived. When he was five he became the elder son, for on 15 November 1897 a third child was born to Sir George and Lady Ida. In memory of an ancestral revenant that he half-believed in, Sir George named his second son Sacheverell.

Sacheverell was as beautiful as Osbert and just as well behaved. Later he wrote of the deep fondness and love that existed between himself and his mother during his earliest years.[5] As for Edith's ill treatment as a child, he ascribed such more to his sister's tendency toward fantasy than fact; yet Osbert, whose childhood memories were always happy in contrast to those of his sister, years later wrote of Edith: "I doubt if any child was more mismanaged by her parents. They failed to comprehend the sort of being who was in the process of flowering before their eyes . . . (*LH,* 110).

The extent that Edith was "mismanaged by her parents" has been discussed by her biographers.[6] While it is true that all her life she hinted at some hideous event, some unforgiveable betrayal by her father and mother, her early years were probably not so wretched as she wanted others to believe. To maintain that she bore psychic scars because she was an unwanted and unloved child, that her earliest years are responsible for a sense of tragedy and loss echoing throughout her entire life, may have a modicum of truth; but a modicum of truth can easily be stretched into error.

That she was an ultrasensitive child is obvious. That she had a power with words to protect herself and to be revenged on anyone who slighted or mistreated her cannot be denied. Still, whether all this justifies certain remarks she made toward the end of her life cannot be taken at face value. In her autobiography, *Taken Care Of,* she wrote: "Perhaps I, at four years old, knew the incipient anguish of the poet I was to become" (*TC,* 16).

Several clichés emphasize twigs being bent and trees so inclined, but just as many bromides have it that good writers must suffer, that every poet is another Prometheus unrewarded and actually punished for his contributions to humanity. More than likely, Edith liked to think of herself as more of a Prometheus than a twig bent out of shape. Even as a child she played the role of the artist. When someone asked her what she would like to be when she grew up, she announced her intention of becoming a genius (*TC,* 17).

Oversimplification is often falsification but, simply put, Edith was an exasperating child who could not be bent or molded to her parents' wishes. They struggled, nonetheless, to make her conform to the conventions of their class. When she wanted to learn to play the piano, for example, they insisted it had to be the cello. When it was discovered she like to read Swinburne's poetry, Sir George demanded that she forego such sensual verse. If she had to read poetry, he pontificated, she should read Tennyson for beauty, Austin Dobson for charm, and Kipling for strength.

To top off everything, there was the "Bastille," as she dubbed a complicated orthopedic device she was forced to wear. "The imprisonment began under my arms," she once complained, "preventing me from resting them on my sides. My legs were also imprisoned to my ankles, and at night these, and the soles of my feet, were locked up in an excruciating contraption" (*TC,* 16). Designed essentially to strengthen and straighten her spine, the "Bastille" apparently did little to correct a slight curvature not uncommon among young girls who grow tall too quickly. In addition, she had to endure a facial brace meant to improve the shape of her aquiline nose.

That Sir George actually mocked the curvature of her back or viciously ridiculed her hawklike nose is more than likely just part of Edith's automythomania. Actually, he did all that could be done for his daughter by taking advantage of expensive orthopedic braces and corsets prescribed by the leading medical specialists of the day.

That a sensitive child might perceive the matter differently is not surprising. Just as the Paris Bastille was symbolic of degrading oppression, so, too, Edith's "Bastille," with its restrictive belts and rectifying buckles, stood for all the slights and cruelties of which she was convinced her parents had been guilty.

Time for Literature

In her teens, Edith devoted much of her time to literature. Poetry in particular became a cause, an activity that took her mind off the "Bastille" and the regimen her parents tried to impose upon her. One of her supreme pleasures at the time was the initiation of Osbert and Sacheverell into the world of the imagination, the realm of art and music. Osbert was highly receptive to all his older sister taught him, and Sacheverell proved to be a perfect pupil. "When she wasn't writing poetry herself," he later noted, "she was reading it to me and encouraging me to write, so that poetry appeared a natural part of life. In those days Edith would have made anyone a poet."[7]

She devoured those English poets she most admired and ignored those who failed to measure up to her critical standards. Years later, when asked to name her favorite author, she responded without a moment's hesitation "Shakespeare."[8] Then she added, "And of course Pope. I used to read *The Rape of the Lock* at night under the bedclothes by the light of a candle. It's a wonder I didn't set myself on fire. I had memorized it by the time I was twelve."[9]

Keats and Wordsworth were other early favorites. As she grew older she came to admire Swinburne, who had been one of her first literary loves, more for sound than substance. When she was fifteen, she undertook without her parents' permission, a pilgrimage to the Isle of Wight, equipped with a vial of honey to pour over Swinburne's grave, upon which she also placed a sprig of flowers.[10]

Browning was a little beyond her. Convinced that he was a great poet, she still found him a bore at times. Elizabeth Barrett Browning was a major disappointment: she thought *Sonnets from the Portuguese* were beautiful in emotion but simply not good sonnets. Mrs. Browning's trouble, Edith complained, was that she was "forever haunted by the shade of her horsehair sofa. She was the kindest and best of women but she had a rare talent for making great things small."[11]And just as Elizabeth Barrett escaped from her father's dominance when Robert Browning came along, Edith dreamed that her escape from her parents' home would occur when an eligible young man came along to rescue her. For the time being, at least, she could carry on a love affair with poetry.

In 1903, when Edith was sixteen, Helen Roothman arrived at Renishaw Hall. This new governess, who was ten years older than her charge, became Edith's first confidante. A close friendship developed between them that endured for more than twenty years, mainly because they shared in common a devotion to literature. Helen's specialty, however, was French poetry, not English, and it was she who introduced Edith to the works of Verlaine, Rimbaud, and Mallarmé. Though Edith had had a taste of Baudelaire through Swinburne's translations of the author of *Les Fleurs du mal,* she found her governess' favorites even more to her liking.

Encouraged by Helen Roothman, Edith crammed notebook after notebook with her own poems. She began to submit them for publication. In March 1913 her first poem, "Drowned Suns," was printed in the *Daily Mirror.* As happy as the event made Edith and Helen, who had become mentor and companion, it troubled Sir George and Lady Ida. They suspected that Edith would now leave Renishaw to follow a literary life of her own in London. And they were right.

Edith feared that it would be impossible for her to be truly creative if she remained at Renishaw Hall. Besides, she was now twenty-six years old. The years had gone by quickly, and it was time to be on her own. If she were to fulfill herself as a poet, Edith reasoned, she had to make a break with Sir George and Lady Ida, but such a step was more than they could fathom. Insinuating ungratefulness on her part, they demanded that she remain. She was just as adamant in her determination to leave. The impasse was resolved in her favor when in April 1913 she and Helen caught a train for London. Osbert had already found temporary lodgings for them in St. Petersburgh Place, Baywater.

In Literary London

Osbert had arrived in London in 1912 as a new subaltern in the Grenadier Guards; as such, he was placed on duty at the Tower of London. After his time at Eton, Osbert hoped to go to Oxford; but Sir George decided that his son should go into the army. That Osbert never wanted to be a soldier meant little to Sir George. After he failed a qualifying examination for Sandhurst, it looked as though Osbert's military career would be over before it began. Sir George exerted influence in the proper quarters, however, and Osbert was commissioned into a crack cavalry regiment stationed at Aldershot.

The life of a hussar had little appeal for Osbert. To be brief, he was not cut out to be a cavalry officer. He detested horses and occasionally fell off them. One day when asked what he thought about horses, he replied that he really preferred giraffes; they had more beautiful lines.[12] After months of boredom and discomfort at Aldershot, he was transferred to the Grenadier Guards. Not only did he no longer have to contend with saddling up every day, but the Grenadiers struck him as being a far more civilized military body. Although he realized that he possessed none of the martial attributes, he appreciated the traditions of the Guards and he enjoyed their privileges.

To begin with, the Grenadiers were usually stationed in London, where they ceremoniously guarded the royal palaces, the Bank of England, and other national institutions. As an officer in the Guards, Osbert had a great deal of free time, which he spent at theaters, art galleries, and concert halls. In the great houses of London, to which he often had himself invited, he encountered the musicians, painters, and writers who were shaping contemporary art. He met Claude Debussy, Frederick Delius, and Richard Strauss. He discussed fiction with George Moore and painting with Henry Tonks. One night in a fashionable drawing room he was introduced to Robert Ross, who had once been Oscar Wilde's close friend; and through Ross, Osbert met almost everyone else of importance in literary London.

Osbert had always hoped to remain a peacetime gentleman-soldier, if he had to be a soldier at all. Unfortunately, in November 1914, shortly after his twenty-second birthday, his regiment was activated. Shortly thereafter, he found himself in France. Two days after he arrived in the front-line trenches, he was handed a letter from his father. Sir George had written to his son to give such advice as: "Directly you hear the first shell, retire . . . to the cellar, and remain there until all firing has ceased. . . . Keep warm and have plenty of plain, nourishing food at frequent but regular intervals. And, of course, plenty of rest"(L, 78). The sheer impracticality of Sir George's suggestions brought a smile to Osbert's lips. Later, during combat, he had little to smile about.

While bivouacked near Ypres, Osbert expressed his sense of the barbarism of war in a short poem entitled "Babel." Remarkably, though surrounded by death and filled with despair, he now found his purpose in life. He realized that he had done more than write a poem; he had become a poet: "some instinct, and a combination of feelings not hitherto experienced, united to drive me to paper" (*L,* 115). Publication of "Babel" in the *London Times* of 11 May 1916 marked Osbert's debut as a man of letters.

The devastation of war experienced at firsthand gave new meaning to the sacredness of art. The artist, Osbert was now convinced, was "a priest, prophet, and law giver, as well as interpreter: the being who enabled men to see and feel and pointed out to them the way" (*L,* 118). Still, he had doubts about his playing the role in earnest. He felt that he had been poorly educated and was not widely read; nevertheless, he knew where he stood: "I would be, for as long as I lived, on the side of the arts."[13]

Discovering Aesthetic Peaks

Unlike Osbert, Sacheverell, though shy and retiring by nature, had no doubts about his aesthetic bent. Edith had sparked his early interest in poetry, and Sir George first awakened his younger son's devotion to architecture and painting. "Even when I was very young," Sacheverell once said, "my father was always talking to me about paintings and buildings he had seen, particulary in southern Italy."[14] By the time he was thirteen, Sacheverell had already embarked upon an ambitious program to discover the artistic peaks of the human spirit. Toward that end, he delved into the lives of poets and painters, architects and musicians.

When Sacheverell was sixteen, he became especially enthralled by the works of Augustus John, Walter Sickert, and Jacob Epstein. After viewing the art of Filippo Marinetti at the Sackville Gallery, he read the artist's manifesto "Art and Literature," in which the doctrine of futurism was boldly proclaimed: the time had come to blow up all museums in order to overcome the stultifying influence of the past. But it was readily apparent to young Sacheverell that Marinetti was a fanatic. How could Sacheverell become a connoisseur of traditional beauty if all the art of the past were destroyed?

At Eton, Sacheverell had his own quarters, got on well with his teachers and classmates, and read everything he could get his eyes into. He was such an excellent student, unlike Osbert, that Sir George could not deny him matriculation at Oxford. In the meantime, Osbert, who was enjoying the artistic milieu of London, began to introduce his younger brother to all the worthwhile personalities he had already met, the writers, the painters, the musicians; and having become a balletomane, he made certain to introduce Sacheverell to the great Diaghilev. After viewing several performances of the Ballets Russes, Sacheverell became as enthusiastic a devotee of the dance as his brother Osbert.

Nor had Edith neglected her younger brother. She always had great faith in his lyric gift, and now she actively encouraged him to experiment with verse. "Perhaps in my case," Sacheverell wrote, "I was as much a pupil of my sister as any poet had ever been of another."[15] Osbert gave equal encouragement. If they survived the war, Osbert promised, they would live together, create together. Both had lost several close friends in combat and one worried about the other, especially since Sacheverell now also had a commission in the Special Reserve of the Grenadiers. But Sacheverell was not to see combat and Osbert was invalided home from France with a serious case of blood poisoning.

For Osbert and Sacheverell the war had lain "across the years like a wound that never heals."[16] When peace was finally declared in November 1918, they agreed to turn their attention to worthwhile matters. First, however, Osbert had to put his days as a soldier behind him. As soon as news of his demobilization reached him, he ritualized his return to civilian life by launching his uniform out to sea in a hamper and by having his bearskin made into a muff for his housekeeper. Now he and Sacheverell could apply themselves to literature.

Edith, who had been in London for five years, stood ready and eager to offer her assistance. London, too, would be Osbert's and Sacheverell's base of operations. Along with Edith, who delighted to play hostess, they entertained dozens of new friends, among them Virginia Woolf, T. S. Eliot, D. H. Lawrence, Harold Acton, Clive Bell, Lytton Strachey, Maurice Ravel, and George Gershwin. Being in the company of such creative individuals, sharing their thoughts and learning of their aspirations, served as a further stimulus for Edith, Osbert, and Sacheverell. They were ready now to take all necessary steps to realize their own aesthetic dreams.

As the years went on, Edith developed into a poet of great emotional depth, dedicated to sincere human concerns. Osbert gained fame as a writer of fiction, an essayist who tilted at the windmills of the literary and art establishment, and the author of one of the finest autobiographies of the century. Sacheverell, perhaps the most erudite of the three, followed his own interests and wrote poetically insightful studies of music, art, and architecture in a rich and rhythmic prose.

The stream of the trio's creativity seemed perpetual. Over a fifty-year period, they produced almost 200 volumes of poetry, fiction, music, art, and literary criticism; and they contributed just under 1,000 essays, articles, translations, and musical settings to a multitude of books and periodicals. Virtually all they wrote, it must be added, was a consequence of their life experiences. To ignore such factors, for example, as Edith's religious conversion, or Osbert's military service, or Sacheverell's travels to all parts of the globe—or their theories of art, the influence they had on each other, the response of the critics—in a consideration of their works is simply impossible.

Final Wishes

Edith died on 9 December 1964. In accordance with her wishes, a funeral mass was said for her at Farm Street Church in London. An ecumenical service was conducted by a Roman Catholic priest and the Anglican vicar of the parish. Burial followed in the graveyard at Weedon Lois, near Weston, not far from Sacheverell's home in Northamptonshire. Today a Henry Moore sculpture depicting the hand of a young child clasping the hand of an old man—an obvious symbol of the continuity of life through each generation—marks her grave. Lettered into the stone are lines from Edith's "Wind of Early Spring":

> The past and the present are as one—
> Accordant and discordant, youth and age,
> And death and birth. For out of one comes all—
> From all comes one.

Osbert took the news of Edith's passing calmly, though he feared he soon would follow his sister in death. On 4 May 1969 he did so. In accordance with his wishes, after an Anglican ceremony for the dead, his body was cremated and the ashes buried in a Protestant cemetery outside his estate in Montefugoni, Italy. He had once requested that a copy of his first and favorite novel, *Before the Bombardment,* be interred with him, and it was duly placed in his urn. What the final wishes and requests, as of this writing, of Sacheverell—the last surviving member of the Sitwell trio—may be are known only to his immediate family.

Chapter Two

Beyond Surface Meaning

Wheels

The Sitwells served a literary apprenticeship in the founding and editing of their own periodical—*Wheels,* the first number of which appeared in 1916. Edith had already published at her own expense a small booklet of verse, *The Mother and Other Poems* (1915), and contributed several poems to various periodicals and newspapers. Osbert had also published several of his poems, and he was represented with Edith in a volume entitled *Twentieth Century Harlequin-ade and Other Poems* (1916). Sacheverell, who was only nineteen at the time, soon followed his brother and sister into print. In the meantime, the trio all worked toward a common goal and still encouraged one another to the best of which each was individually capable.

"In the beginning they were three *enfants terribles,*" Frank Swinnerton once commented. "Being excluded, either by their own act or by the repulsion of the editorial canon from 'Georgian Poetry,' they established a counter blast to which they gave the name 'Wheels.' "[1] The Sitwells, it is true, launched their periodical in opposition to a series of collections of Georgian verse that began in 1912. *Georgian Poetry* irritated the Sitwell's sensibilities.

They detested, in particular, the simplistic narratives about romantic love, the faithfulness of dogs, the chirping of birds, and the wholesomeness of all life—invariably done in conventional metrics—that frequently appeared between the covers of this popular anthology. There was so much inferior verse in *Georgian Poetry* that even an occasional good poem by Walter de la Mare, John Drinkwater, John Masefield, or one of the other figures now dubbed "Georgian" was ignored by the Sitwells. There was something false about Georgian "realism," they complained, with its emphasis on optimism, moral subjects, and common speech patterns. They determined an antidote was necessary.

Nancy Cunard's poem "Wheels," which was published in the

13

first issue, gave the Sitwells their central thrust and a name for their new publication. "I sometimes think that all our thoughts are wheels," she had written, "rolling forever through the painted world/ Moved by the cunning of a thousand clowns."

Edith, Osbert, and Sacheverell worked on and contributed to each issue, and though Edith was the prime mover she did not label herself editor until the 1918 number.[2] *Wheels* became an annual event, lasting six numbers, until 1921. Aldous Huxley, Arnold James, Iris Tree, and many other poets contributed their latest poems; but since most of them were neophytes and relatively unknown, *Wheels* failed to capture many readers. It evoked the rage of the critics, however.

Today it is difficult to understand the vituperative frenzy of some of the first reviewers of *Wheels*. For the Sitwells to be denounced as weird verbal experimenters was one thing, but to be castigated for various aesthetic, political, and social views they never seriously entertained, to be derided for writing poetry conceived in morbid eccentricity and executed in factitious gloom, was another. And yet to earn the contempt of limited critics and feel the scorn of Philistines was an achievement in itself, they reasoned. They were especially amused by a parody that appeared in a publication called *Cranks*, with poems by Obert, Sebert, and Ethelberta Standstill.

At first they tried to remain aloof and to disregard their obtuse critics. Finding this next to impossible, they began to write clever and cutting ripostes. The 1919 issue of *Wheels*, for example, contains an open letter in which they take to task one carping critic. Though they claimed to like her personally, and detected in her attack upon them "less of the cloven hoof than of a certain wooden head," they could not quite grasp why she was indifferent to "skilled technique in poetry." Poetasters, they protested, they were not. They preferred to draw a veil over the entire painful scene, but warned: "Frankly, darling, what a stinker. Don't do it again, *please*. . . . "[3]

The Sitwells could ably defend themselves, and they did so with glee; still, they were pleased when the abusive hubbub found in several reviews of *Wheels* evoked a few sympathetic voices. Arnold Bennett's was one. To him, the Sitwells were clever and stimulating and not wrong in their open defiance of poetic convention. "The Sitwells can all write," he proclaimed. "Further, they all afflict the public—I mean the poetic public—which is a grand thing to do. They exult in a scrap. Battle is in the curve of their nostrils."[4]

However much the publication of *Wheels* actually "afflicted" the poetic public is open to debate, but the Sitwells, in their own iconoclastic fashion, were doing for twentieth-century literature what several of their most creative contemporaries were likewise doing. The names of T. S. Eliot, James Joyce, and D. H. Lawrence come immediately to mind. The same spirit of modernity discernible in "The Love Song of J. Alfred Prufrock," *The Portrait of the Artist as a Young Man,* and *The Rainbow*—all written about the same time the Sitwells were experimenting with their verse—nucleated *Wheels.*

Significance of Love

One of the most significant poems published in *Wheels* is Edith's "The Mother."[5] Privately published in 1915 in only 500 copies, she believed it deserved another printing. A long narrative of more than 160 lines, its theme is obvious, its plot direct. A woman is murdered by her son. Greed and sex are responsible for the matricide. A bit of gold hidden beneath the woman's bed is filched by her son to entertain his paramour. The mother's heart speaks:

> Young girl, you dance and laugh to see
> The thing that I have come to be.
> Oh, once this heart was like your own!
> Go, pray that yours may not turn to stone.
>
> This is the murdered heart of one
> Who bore and loved an only son.
> For him, I worked away mine eyes:
> My starved breast could not still his cries. . . .
>
> I had put by a little gold
> To bury me when I was cold.
> That fanged wanton kiss to but,
> My son's love willed that I should die.

After the bloody deed, the mother's spirit cannot rest, for though her son slew her with "a wicked knife flashed serpent-wise," she believes she hears him weep over what he has done:

> They say the Dead may never dream.
> But yet I heard my pierced heart scream

His name in the dark. They lie
Who say the Dead can ever die.

For in the grave I may not sleep,
For dreaming that I hear him weep.
And in the dark my dead hands grope
In search of him. O barren hope!

Loyal even beyond the grave, her maternal instinct makes her protest the fault was hers: "All mine, all mine the sin. The love/I bore him was not deep enough." Obvious in such taut lines and the melodramatic aspects of the poem is the theme of complete and unquestioning love.

Edith played upon this theme of unquestioning love in a few of the other half-dozen or so pieces in *The Mother and Other Poems.* In "The King of China's Daughter," the second poem in the collection, she wrote "She never would love me/Though I hung my cap and bells upon/Her nut meg tree." A nursery rhyme of sorts, this poem, both light and serious as nursery rhymes usually are, allows a reader to question why a cap and bells were hung on a nut meg tree to begin with, or why "The King of China's daughter/Pretended not to see." More important than meaning, perhaps, is the poem's obvious dictional pattern; for Edith was apparently as much taken up with a prissy, doll-house world full of such exotica as tambourines, mandolines, parakeets, and chinoiserie as she was interested in the theme of love.

At the time, moreover, fascinated by what she labeled "sense-transfusion," Edith began to use the language of one sense "to pierce down to the essence of the thing seen, by discovering in it attributes which at first sight appear alien," but which are acutely related— "by producing its quintessential colour . . . sharper, brighter than that seen by an eye grown stale. . . ."(*TC,* xxxii).

From a technical point of view, the third poem in the collection, "Serenade," is one of the best:

The tremulous gold of stars within your hair
Are yellow bees flown from the hive of night,
Finding the blossom of your eyes more fair
Than all the pale flowers folded from the light.
Then, Sweet, awake, and ope your dreaming eyes
Ere those bright bees have flown and darkness dies.

Note how the music of evening, the primacy of darkness, is established in the opening couplet. In attributing the sun's color to the stars, she recommends a causative relationship between darkness and light, night and day. The yellow bees, born from the mothering hive of night, experience the darkness of the evening world and find blossoms of the eyes of the beloved more fair than "all the pale flowers folded from the light." And the concluding couplet pleads that the loved one open dreaming eyes before the bright bees have departed and darkness is overcome by light.

Most of the poems in *Clowns' Houses,* which followed in 1918, and *The Wooden Pegasus,* published two years later, are similar in form and theme to those in *The Mother and Other Poems.* The poems comprising *Bucolic Comedies* (1923), most of which date from the early twenties, are more experimental and deal less with exotica than with rhythm. Most of the bucolic poems, admittedly, may seem comedic nonsense, but a careful reading indicates that their strained language and odd images serve a serious purpose.

In "Aubade," for example, Edith depicts the sad stupidity of a servant girl on a country farm rising from her bed and coming down to light a morning fire.

> Jane, Jane
> Tall as a crane,
> The morning light creaks down again;
>
> Comb your cockscomb-ragged hair,
> Jane, Jane, come down the stair.
>
> Each dull wooden stalactite
> Of rain creaks, hardened by the light,
>
> Sounding like an overtone
> From some lonely world unknown.
>
> But the creaking empty light
> Will never harden into sight.
>
> Will never penetrate your brain
> With overtones of blunt rain.

The dawn "creaks" about Jane in the third line because, as Edith once explained, early light does not run smoothly: "it falls in hard cubes, squares, and triangles, which again, give one the impression of a creaking sound, because of the association with wood."[6] The image, though clearly visual, she prefers to render as audile, in keeping with Rimbaud's "derangement of senses" with which she was familiar from a close reading of his poetry. As an audile image, "creaks" anticipates the sound of the stairs in line 5 as Jane descends, as well as the sound made by branches of trees, in line 6 that are straining in the wind and rain. And once more there is "creaking empty light" in the tenth line:

> The light would show (if it could harden)
> Eternities of kitchen garden,
>
> Cockscomb flowers that none will pluck,
> And wooden flowers that 'gin to cluck.
>
> In the kitchen you must light
> Flames as staring, red and white,
>
> As carrots or turnips, shining
> Where the cold dawn light lies whining.
>
> Cockscomb hair on the cold wind
> Hangs limp, turns the milk's weak mind. . . .
>
> Jane, Jane
> Tall as a crane,
> The morning light creaks down again!

Facing daily chores of weeding in the garden, Jane feels the flowers there cluck and mock her. The flowers "cluck," apparently, because they are cockscombs. The flames of the fire remind her of the carrots and turnips she has to clean, cut, and cook. Her spirits hang limp as "the milk's weak mind." The concluding triplet echoes the first three lines and emphasizes the endless, boring days of a servant girl.

Like many of Edith's early poems, "Aubade" contains recollections of her own childhood. Thinking of the servant girl Jane brings to the poet's mind, as she noted later, "the shivering movement of a certain cold dawn light upon the floor," which became suggestive of "high animal whining or whimpering, a half-frightened and subservient urge to something outside our consciousness."[7]

A few technical experiments in *Bucolic Comedies,* in addition to those of rhythm, were meant mainly to suggest a dronelike sound, like that of a hive or the wind in the trees. Some of the poems, Edith explained, were to have "a goat-footed, rustic sound, deliberately uncouth," so that it would seem as "if we are not listening to the peasants' boots falling on a soft soil but to the far earlier sound of satyr hooves falling on a ground that is hard with winter, or harsh and sharp with spring, or mad and harsh with summer. . . ."[8]

Most readers of Edith's *Bucolic Comedies* rightfully complained that effective poems did not require explanations of their prosody or profundity. Professional critics tended to ignore the work; the few who concerned themselves with it were less than enthusiastic. One critic, nevertheless, felt that *Bucolic Comedies* was an accomplished collection. "As a realization of artifice in poetry, from their metrical virtuosity, to evocative music," he effused, *"Bucolic Comedies* is one of the most astounding and revolutionary volumes of modern verse."[9] At best, his was a minority opinion.

Assiduous Application

During the same period that Edith was experimenting with her *Clowns' Houses* and *Bucolic Comedies,* Osbert began to apply himself assiduously to controversial journalism, art criticism, and the writing of poetry. Under the pseudonym "Miles," he contributed a series of satirical poems to the *Spectator* and the *Nation.* Several of his tendentious essays on warmongering, armchair generals, and the complete folly of armed combat began to appear in various newspapers, especially the *Daily Herald.*

As busy as he was with the written word, Osbert still had time for the visual arts. To fill the vacuum the war left in the artistic life of London, in 1919 he and Sacheverell mounted a controversial exhibition of avant-garde art at the Mansard Gallery. At this first important exhibition of French art held since the beginning of the war, they placed on exhibit canvases of Matisse, Utrillo, Picasso, Dufy, Derain, and Modigliani and the sculptures of Zadkine and Archipenko. The exhibition, the most representative of contemporary art seen in London for several years, established the Sitwell brothers as impresarios of art and important proponents of the modern movement.

About the same time, Osbert became joint editor with Herbert Read of a new quarterly, *Arts and Letters,* and in this capacity he, accompanied by Sacheverell, traveled to Fiume to interview Gabriele D'Annunzio. The Sitwell brothers were not above hero worship, and they were intent upon meeting the poet-soldier they regarded as another Byron. Had not D'Annunzio, an artist with roots in the aestheticism of the nineties, entered into open rebellion against the Italian government and set himself up as the "Regent of Carnaro" at Fiume? Had he not, moreover, proclaimed the sanctity of art and established music as the official religion of the short-lived republic?[10]

Of greater importance than D'Annunzio's influence upon the Sitwells and Osbert's editorials for *Arts and Letters* was his completion of a book of more than fifty poems, many of which had already appeared in *Wheels,* the *Nation,* and the *Cambridge Magazine.* Osbert entitled his first verse collection *Argonaut and Juggernaut.* Publication of *Twentieth Century Harlequinade* (1916), a collection of poems by Edith and himself, and *The Winstonburg Line* (1919), a satirical attack on England's plan to put down Bolshevism in Russia, had first brought Osbert's name before a small group of poetry readers. And now they took readily to his *Argonaut and Juggernaut.*

"How Shall We Rise to Greet the Dawn," the volume's preface poem, served as an excellent epigraph. Osbert had written the piece mainly to memorialize the Armistice. As a dedicated singer of a new day he would "cast down the idols of a thousand years." Accordingly, he urged all poets to

> . . . prune the tree of language
> Of its dead fruit.
> Let us melt up the clichés
> Into molten metal,
> Fashion weapons that will scald and flay;
> Let us curb this eternal humour
> And become witty.
> Let us dig up dragon's teeth
> From this fertile soil
> Swiftly,
> Before they fructify;
> Let us give them as medicine
> To the writhing monster itself.

In the poems that followed, he gave expression to the two great issues that obsessed him at the time. One was the stupidity of war;

the other, the need to establish a new and just society. Both he and Sacheverell were socialistically inclined at the time and were sympathetic to the revolutionaries in Russia. "My brother and I admired the Bolshiviks," he later commented, "especially since they put a stop to a war that had become for the Russian troops, left without arms, a shambles" (*L,* 10). Communism was fine for the Soviet Union, Osbert and Sacheverell often proclaimed, though they never went so far as to favor it for Britain. Herbert Read, who saw through the Sitwell's political extremism, was moved to remark that there was "a lot of pose in their revolt."[11]

Actually, there was little to quarrel with in most of *Argonaut and Juggernaut,* but Osbert's fervent idealism and politically pink sentiments irritated critics who read his views on war and society as invective. In "World-Hymn to Moloch," "The Blind Pedlar," and "Sheep Song," he gave vent to what could easily be read as less than patriotic expression.

During the war he had written "World-Hymn to Moloch" to satirize man's quest for victory on the battlefield. In this poem, the sun "lives under a heap and hills of dead," but the god of battle is still praised and petitioned:

> Eternal Moloch, strong to slay,
> Do not seek to heal or save.
> Lord, it is the better way,
> Swift to send them to the grave. . . .

> Cast on us thy crimson smile
> Moloch, lord, we pray to thee,
> Send at least one victory. . . .

Shortly after the war ended, Osbert wrote "The Blind Pedlar," in which a poor man who used to bemoan his lack of vision now thanks God that he cannot see

> —The young men crippled, old and sad,
> With faces burnt and torn away;
> Or those who, rich and old;
> Have battened on the slaughter,
> Whose faces, gorged with blood and gold,
> Are creased in purple laughter!

In "Sheep Song," the flock declares, "There are no sheep like us./ We come from an imperial bleat." They behold blood "drip and ooze on the walls" of the world, and they do nothing when their lambs are fattened for slaughter. Their ovine minds hold "all the secrets of the vacuum." Only when the head sheep bleats are they moved to action, and

> When he stampedes
> —Heavy with foot-rot—
> We gallop after him
> Until
> In our frenzy
> We trip him up
> —And a new sheep leads us.

When they stampede, they convince themselves it is a noble thing to do; but their stampede does little but exhaust them. Foolishly they reason:

> We are stampeding to end stampedes.
> We are fighting for lambs
> Who are never likely to be born.
> When once a sheep gets its blood up
> The goats will remember. . . .

Finally a herdsman has to swoop down on the silly sheep and force them to return to their pens.

One critic out of sympathy with the strident sentiments of "World-Hymn to Moloch," "The Blind Pedlar," "Sheep Song," and several other satirical poems complained that the sole impressive feature of *Argonaut and Juggernaut* was its title. Its satire, he claimed, was oratorical and offensive. A few poems produced unexpected shocks of delight, but they were too few to matter. He dismissed the volume as coming from a neophyte who was "one of the . . . exponents of the modern manner, who seems as yet to be uncertain both of his aim and method."[12]

Another critic, equally unimpressed with *Argonaut and Juggernaut,* remarked that Osbert had been moved to write the volume more by unbelief in the ideals of others rather than by the passionate force of his own ideals: "He is a sceptic, not a sufferer. His work proceeds less from his heart than from his brain."[13] Favorable criticism came from a reviewer who found passages in the poems that demonstrated Osbert had "embryonic talent that may develop significantly." First, he recommended, the poet had to get rid of his "flaming indignation and scorn."[14]

Another Satirical Work

To rid himself of some of the venom that had built up during the war years, Osbert wrote another satirical work, *At the House of Mrs. Kinfoot* (1921). In this series of poems he struck at the British middle class. Their smugness and feelings of superiority had been to a great extent responsible for England's going to war. Worse yet, it seemed to him that they had been eager to keep the conflagration going. During the two years he spent in the trenches, there was little he could do to advocate his own position of working toward a negotiated peace.

In one of the more acerbic poems, "At the Foot of the Ladder," he observed

> Listen, then, to the gospel of Mrs. Kinfoot:
> "The world was made for the British Bourgeoisie,
> They are the Swiss Family Robinson;
> The world is not what it was.
> We cannot understand all this unrest. . . .
> The war was splendid, wasn't it?
> Oh yes, splendid, splendid."
>
> Mrs. Kinfoot is a dear,
> And so artistic.

Osbert left little doubt about his contempt for the dullness and complacency of the middle class. More with bitterness than humor he wrote that

> The British Bourgeoisie
> Is not born,
> And does not die,
> But, if it is ill,
> It has a frightened look in its eye.

A poem entitled "Malgré Soi" brings *At the House of Mrs. Kinfoot* to a close. In a lighter vein Osbert has the parvenu Mrs. Kinfoot expire. On her way to heaven she plans a dinner party there for all her important friends, but she soon learns that most of them, "the Counsellors and Kings/And brilliant bearers of a famous name," have already been dispatched to hell. Realizing that she will not be among such prominent individuals, she cries out: "I swear I beat my children. . . . I will tell/How I escaped a Ducal Co-respondent/Last year—my God—I must insist on Hell." But despite her earnest pleas, Mrs. Kinfoot is made part of the heavenly choir. Whenever she tries to join her friends in the great abyss, "to flee/To that perpetual party down below," the angels stop her. "Dear Mrs. Kinfoot," they protest, "You are good!—We know!"

In the same year that *At the House of Mrs. Kinfoot* was published, Osbert wrote his first critical essay, *Who Killed Cock Robin?* As a young poet, somewhat uncertain of his art, he wrote the essay principally to formulate his own thoughts on literature. Familiar with Jean Cocteau's celebrated tract on art and music, *Le Coq et l'Arlequin* (1918), Osbert echoed some of its view in *Wheels*. In *Who Killed Cock Robin?* he made use of what he had borrowed from Cocteau and added his own squibs on what was wrong with contemporary poetry. He had been especially offended by those who had written of "larks singing in the trenches," those poets who had glorified war.

"Poetry," he objected, "is *not* the monopoly of lark-lovers or those who laud the Nightjay, any more than it belongs to the elephant or the macaw!"[15] Those who sentimentalized poetry and wrote to please Philistines were simple versifiers who missed what was vital and crucial to record their own shallow ecstasies. More often than not, these "mammon poets," as he labeled them, were academics intent upon placing "daisy chains and cowslip bells on the tomb of Victorian poetry in the hope that the corpse would miraculously revive" (*W,* 6). Obviously, he had in mind the Georgian poets who scrawled "sentimental observations . . . about that . . . matter-of-fact old hag, Nature" (*W,* 6). True poets, he maintained, had a far more important mission.

The problem was that so many scribblers of verse did not know the meaning of poetry. For all those who did not, Osbert supplied a definition: "Poetry is the conversation of the gods through the medium of man" (*W,* 29). A poet's responsibility, he held, was to transmit, like wireless apparatus, what the gods say. If such an explanation seemed vaguely transcendental, or too much like Coleridge's views on the aeolian harp, Osbert had another way of trying to explain what poetry is. "Poetry," he added, "is like . . . a crystal globe, with Truth imprisoned in it, like a fly in amber" (*W*, 6).

Obviously, Edith and Sacheverell concurred with everything Osbert had to say about the subject. For them, *Who Killed Cock Robin?* was a brilliant manifesto on poetry, an excellent put-down of the Georgian poets, a clever polemic that defended the modern movement. *Who Killed Cock Robin?* said all the important things about the kind of poetry the Sitwells themselves were writing.

Chapter Three
Facade: A Joint Effort

Instant Notoriety

Despite the controversial nature of *The Mother and Other Poems, Clowns' Houses, The Wooden Pegasus,* and *Bucolic Comedies,* Edith's early volumes of poetry, though they disturbed certain critics, caught the attention of a limited number of readers. This changed with her public recitation of *Facade* on 12 June 1923. Overnight she became a celebrity, a poet to reckon with, though this was not the first time *Facade* had been performed. It had been presented privately before an invited audience some sixteen months earlier.

Friends at the first private recitation were enthusiastic both before and after Edith's performance. They approved of most of the poems, and they especially enjoyed the music William Walton had written for the occasion. The suggestion that Edith should write the lyrics and Walton the music had come from Osbert and Sacheverell. At the time they were Walton's closest friends and he was sharing lodgings with them. *Facade* was therefore a joint effort of Edith and Walton, of Osbert and Sacheverell.

The work came into being chiefly because of technical experiments with prosody that Edith was conducting at the time. Fascinated by the transcendental études of Franz Liszt, in which the composer had written music to cover virtually every pianistic complexity possible, she decided to write equally difficult poems with assorted rhythms, including those of the waltz, the fox trot, the polka, the mazurka, the tango, the pasadoblé, and country and sailor dances. Most of her études, accordingly, were inquiries into the nature of rhythm, speed, rhymes, assonance, and dissonance. In addition, she wanted to explore the effect that various impressions have upon the senses and to what extent she could capture notational images.

In his autobiographical volume *Laughter in the Next Room,* Osbert recorded various details about the genesis and composition of *Facade.* As for exactly what aspects of the finished product, he, Sacheverell, Edith, or Walton had contributed, he could not recall; for they

26

were all continually in one another's company as the work took shape and grew in size and scope. When it came time to bestow a title upon their efforts, they made use of a snide remark someone had passed about Edith: "Very clever, no doubt—but what is she but a facade" (*L,* 192). The choice of title was also meant to imply that though something at first glance may appear to have only surface meaning, closer inspection and reflection may reveal far more.

Rumors of the nature of *Facade* had reached the literary world, and at 3:15 in the afternoon of 12 June 1923 a large and curious crowd was present in London's Aeolian Hall. Those at this first public performance did not react the same way the Sitwells' friends had done at the private recitation. Indeed, virtually everything about the first public performance provoked controversy.

To begin with, Edith sat with her back to the audience, barely visible behind a transparent curtain adorned with a rather crudely painted moonface. The purported purpose of the curtain and Edith's sitting backward was to allow the audience to concentrate chiefly upon the auditory qualities of the poems. The moonface was in keeping with the dreamlike world of apes, ducks, grotesque lords and ladies, clowns, peasants, and servant girls she had written about.

Sacheverell, who stage-managed the performance, suggested that Edith's voice needed magnification in order to be heard above Walton's music, so he recommended an instrument called a Senger-phone, which had been named after its inventor, George Senger. A Swiss opera singer, Senger first used such an instrument to approximate the voice of a dragon. Osbert, acting as impresario, announced each poem, which Edith then half spoke, half chanted. Out of the Sengerphone, which was made of compressed grasses meant to retain the purity of magnified tonal quality, came such baffling words as "The sound of the onycha/When the phoca has the pica/In the palace of the Queen Chinee!"

Music may have power to sooth the savage breast—and there was little adverse reaction to Walton's orchestration—but the response to Edith's poetry bordered on the primitive.[1] There was a bit of polite applause from certain members of the audience, friends of the Sitwells, no doubt; but the general reaction was hostile. Noel Coward, for one, walked out.[2] Most of the audience stayed, mainly out of curiosity, wondering what might happen next. They did not have long to wait; for after the performance, some of those who endured the entire recitation became so threatening that Edith was cautioned to remain on stage behind the curtain. Someone whispered to her that one old lady was waiting to thrash her with an umbrella.

Disgruntled spectators who had purchased tickets more to see and to be seen than to listen complained they were victims of a hoax. They had gone to Aeolian Hall, presumably, to hear a bit of music and some simplistic verse. What they heard sounded like gibberish. Had they listened more attentively they might have discovered—in addition to a great deal of humor and gaiety—subtle criticisms of modern life, innuendoes of despair, decay, and death.

Never were more brickbats hurled at a poet. In the press Edith and her brothers were attacked as ostentatious fools, eccentric avant-garde iconoclasts, and worse. For several weeks subsequently, Osbert complained, they were obliged to go about London feeling as though they had committed murder: "When we entered a room, there would fall a sudden, unpleasing hush. Even friends avoided catching one's eye, and if the very word *facade* was breathed, there would ensue a stampede for other subjects" (*L,* 186).

Virtuoso Exercises

By way of defense, it should be pointed out that when Edith wrote *Facade* she had come to believe that a change in the direction, imagery, and rhythms of poetry had become necessary, owing, as she put it, "to the rhythmical flaccidity, the verbal deadness, the dull and expected patterns" of contemporary verse (*TC,* 123). The poems in *Facade,* consequently, are in many cases virtuoso exercises in verbalizing, studies in rhythmical technicalities. "Fox Trot," "Waltz," and "Hornpipe" are excellent examples of her rhythmical technique; these poems in particular consist of unique experiments into the effect that rhythm has on meaning.

Part of her experimentation sought for effects that speed had on equivalent syllables. Using one trisyllabic word, she discovered, had greater rapidity than three monosyllabic words. The use of two rhymes placed immediately together at the end of each of two lines, furthermore, would be like "leaps in the air." In "Fox Trot," for example, she wrote: "Sally, Mary, Mattie, what's the matter, why cry?/The huntsman and the reynard-coloured sun and I sigh."

Other experiments were made to discover the influence of thickening and thinning, sharpening and softening, of consonants, as in certain lines of "Waltz": "The stars in their apiaries, / Sylphs in their aviaries. . . . " These lines in turn are followed by others that end at times with a dissonance, other times a rhyme. To produce a waltz rhythm she used disyllabic rhymes to begin as well as to end lines, "Daisy and Lily,/Lazy and silly," followed by two long lines with assonances: "Walk by the shore of the wan grassy sea—/Talking once more 'neath a swan-bosomed tree."

In a long preface to *Facade* Edith attempted to rebut anticipated protests and complaints, but even those willing to accept her prosodic theories were still troubled by her startling imagery. Such conceits as "wan grassy sea," "swan-bosomed tree," "foam-bell of ermine," and "asses' milk of stars," she maintained, were partly the result of condensations where the language of one sense was insufficient to cover meaning or sensation. The use of such imagery, she hoped, would express the essence of the thing seen, revealing attributes that at first sight might appear alien to an unresponsive eye or jaded ear.

Perhaps the chief reason *Facade* was so widely misunderstood was that Edith had experimented too freely with abstract patterns. Then, too, the apparent vacuity of some of the poems made them suspect. They seemed meaningless. They were butterflies. But even butterflies, she retorted, can adorn the world and delight the beholder.

Much to her credit, no two poems in *Facade* are alike; indeed, they differ radically one from another. "Hornpipe," for example, is a jaunty piece set to nautical music:

> Sailors come
> To the drum
> Out of Babylon;
> Hobby horses
> Foam, the dumb
> Sky rhinoceros-glum
> Watched the courses of the breakers' rocking horses and with Glaucis,
> Lady Venus on the settee of the horsehair sea. . . .
>
> And the borealic iceberg; floating on they see
> New-arisen Madam Venus for whose sake from far
> Came the fat and zebra'd emperor from Zanzibar
> Where like golden bouquets lay far Asia, Africa, Cathay,
> All laid before that shady lady by the fibroid Shah. . . .
>
> Queen Victoria sitting upon the rocking-horse
> Of a wave said . . . "This minx of course

Is as sharpe as any lynx and blacker-deeper than the drinks and quite as
    Hot as any hottentot, without remorse!
             For the minx,"
             Said she,
             "And the drinks,
             You can see
    Are hot as any hottentot and not the goods for me!"

"Trio for Two Cats" has more than an amusing title; its fast
rhythm creates an eerie mood accentuated with castenets. "I Like
to Do Beside the Seaside" is set to a tango rhythm. "Scotch Rhap-
sody" begins with "Do not take a bath in Jordan, Gordon," and a
heavy drum beat sounds throughout. "Polka" has clever running
rhymes like "Robinson Crusoe rues so" and "The poxy, doxy dear."
"Popular Song" is a joyful and carefree lyric about "Lily O'Grady/
Silly and Shady,/Longing to be/A lazy lady."
    Certain parts of "The Wind's Bastinado" are obvious examples
of nimble sounds that carry little meaning:

          "Buy for a patacoon—
          Sir, you must buy!"
          Said Il Magnifico
          Pulling a fico—
          With a stoccado
          And a gambado,
          Making a wry
          Face: "This corraceous
          Round orchidaceaous
          Fruit is a lie."

"Sir Beelzebub" contains other dazzling displays of sound, but
this poem, unlike "The Wind's Bastinado," suggests several levels
of meaning. The title character begins by calling for

      his syllabub in the hotel in Hell
      Where Proserpine first fell,
      Blue as the gendarmerie were the waves of the sea,
      (Rocking and shocking the barmaid).

      Nobody comes to give him his rum but the
      Rim of the sky hippopotamus-glum
      Enhances the chances to bless with a benison.

Apparently a mockery of the Victorians, the poem singles out their poet laureate:

> Alfred Lord Tennyson crossing the bar laid
> With cold vegetation from pale deputations
> Of temperance workers (all signed In Memoriam)
> Hoping with glory to trip the Laureate's feet,
> (Moving in classical metres). . . .
>
> Like Balaclava, the lava came down from the
> Roof, and the sea's blue wooden gendarmerie
> Took them in charge while Beelzebub roared for his rum.
> . . . None of them come!

Concepts of Space and Time

Most of the poems in *Facade,* when imaginatively read, reveal considerable meaning. For every one that at first seems inexplicable, there is another not too difficult to fathom.[3] "Mariner Man" serves as a good example. In this short, twelve-line poem, Edith plays with concepts of space and time.

A child fascinated by an old sailor wonders about his strangeness and asks him a question: "What are you staring at, mariner man,/ Wrinkled as sea-sand and old as the sea?" To which he responds:

> Those trains will run over their tails, if they can,
> Snorting and sporting like porpoises! Flee
> The burley, the whirligig wheels of the train,
> As round as the world and as large again,
> Running half the way to Babylon, down
> Through fields of clover to gay Troy town—
> A-puffing their smoke as grey at the curl
> On my forehead as wrinkled as sands of the sea!

Hardly enlightened by the old sailor's answer, the child is at least confronted with an infinitude of space and the conundrum of time. The mystery of dimension is suggested through images of curvature. The round wheels of the train to which he refers run on tracks that apparently return to their point of origin. The engines of the trains puff their smoke in curls as they snort and sport like porpoises arching themselves in water. The trains travel over fields of round clover and somehow through space and time from Babylon to Troy, from the present into the past and back to the present.

Finally, Edith's Ancient Mariner puts a question to the child, to himself, and ultimately to the reader: "But what can that matter to you, my girl?/(And what can that matter to me?)" Irony is manifest. The old sailor's journey though time and space recommends several levels of meaning. The whole complex of human existence is implied in his questions.

The frigid imagery, languid movement, and long vowel sounds in "By the Lake," to take another example of a poem not the least bit difficult to grasp, reinforce the narrative of two estranged lovers attempting to recall a happy past. It begins with deliberate, slow-paced lines: "Across the thick and the pastel snow/Two people go. . . ." One turns to the other and asks: "And do you remember/ When last we wandered this shore?" To which the one questioned answers: "Ah no!/For it is cold-hearted December."

Lamenting that their love has been destroyed, the first sighs:

> Dead, the leaves that like asses' ears hung on the trees
> When last we wandered and squandered joy here;
> Now Midas your husband will listen for these
> Whispers—these tears for joy's bier.

Their love affair obviously terminated when the woman, seeking social position, married for money and, in doing so, froze over her lover's heart and ultimately her own. And now

> . . . as they walk, they seem tall pagodas:
> And all the ropes let down from the cloud
> ring the hard cold bell-buds upon the trees—codas
> Of overtones, ecstasies, grown for love's shroud.

The dozen or so *o* sounds in these lines echo the misery of the lovers, which resonates like a muffled mourn of distant, dull bells, a most appropriate coda for a love that has died.

In "The Drum" the verse conveys a sense of menace, of deepening darkness, through the use of subtle dissonances. The opening lines establish the mood:

> In his tall senatorial
> Black and manorial

> House where decoy-duck
> Dust doth clack—
> Clatter and quack
> To a shadow black.

The words "black," "duck," "clatter," and "quack" with their hard consonants and dead vowels, Edith explained, are "dry as dust, and the deadness of dust is conveyed thus, as also by the dulled dissonance of the *a*'s, of the *u* in 'duck' followed by the crumbling assonance of 'dust.' "[4]

A duck's quacking, she obligingly added, was for her the driest of sounds: "it has a peculiar deadness" (*CP,* xxii). In such Sitwellian fashion she explained other aural qualities of "The Drum." She noted that its essential meaning sprang from the narrative of the Demon of Tedworth, a story about witches and witchcraft told by the seventeenth-century Neoplatonist Joseph Glanville.

> Is it black night?
> Black as Hecate howls a star
> Wolfishly, and whined
> The wind from very far. . . .
>
> Only the goatish snow's locks
> Watch the candles lit by fright
> One by one through the black night. . . .
>
> "I thought I saw the wicked old witch in
> The richest gallipot in the kitchen!"
> A lolloping galloping candle confesses. . . .
>
> Out go the candles one by one
> Hearing the rolling of a drum. . . .
>
> Over the floor I heard it go
> Where the drum rolls up the stair, nor tarries.

All through "The Drum," Walton's music provided the proper beat and appropriate rolls, brilliantly emphasizing Edith's narrative. Unfortunately, critics who set out to tar Edith also besmirched Walton with the same brush; one went so far as to carp that the music "had been collected from the works of the most eccentric of

the ultra-moderns" (*L,* 192). Ernest Newman, one of the more
perceptive contemporary musicologists, felt otherwise. He compli-
mented Walton for his contribution to *Facade* and labeled the composer "a humourous musical talent of the first order."[5] Nothing
quite so good as the music for *Facade* had been heard for a long
time, he went on to say, focusing particularly on Walton's creativity
and orchestrating genius.

In truth, even though Walton scored the work for an
unusual combination of six instruments—flute, cello, trumpet, sax-
ophone, clarinet, and percussion—his music did not disturb most
of those at the first public performance of *Facade.* Edith's rushing
delivery and prosodic pyrotechnics did.

Osbert had forewarned the audience that they might not be able
to catch all the words. They heard Osbert clearly enough; but when
they had trouble hearing Edith, they conveniently forgot what Osbert had said. Ernest Newman did not; he claimed that some of the
poems were actually improved by one not being able to catch every
word. The important thing, he suggested, was that the poems did
not have to be read as ordinary verse but required sledge-hammer
insistence on certain words. "The music, the words, the megaphone
and the piquant phrasing of the lines . . . were as much of each
other's bone and flesh as the words and the music are of one in
Tristan or *Pelléas,*" he insisted.[6]

Newman's words pleased Edith, of course, but she still thought
it necessary to rebut the statements of detractors by supplying long,
instructive analyses of individual poems. "Said King Pompey," she
was kind enough to explain, was built upon "a scheme of R's . . .
to produce a faint fluttering sound, like dust fluttering from the
ground, or as the beat of a dying heart" (*CP,* xviii). There are
obvious *R* sounds in the opening lines: "Said King Pompey, the
emperor's ape, / Shuddering black in his temporal cape / of
dust. . . ." But to what extent, it is reasonable to ask, do the *R*'s
suggest "dust fluttering from the ground"? Edith would respond
by expatiating upon affective language and synaesthetic exchange.
A reader willing to consider the poem with an open mind will
appreciate her technical experimentation with synaesthesia, but
whether he will affirm her theories about echo and meaning is
another matter.

Once a reader accepts Edith's theory of *R* sounds, moreover, he
is asked to consider other aural impressions. Certain words ending

in *ck,* she would go on, "cast little imperceptible shadows" (*CP,* xvii). In "The Bat" she played upon such words as "black," "quack," "duck," and "clack." The reason: to contrast shadows "so small yet so menacing, with . . . flat and shadeless words that end with *t* and *d*" (*CP,* xvii). Some of the *a*'s she contended, have neither depth nor body, are flat and death-rotten, though at times the words in which they occur cast a small menacing shadow because of the *ck* ending, and frequently these shadows are followed almost immediately by latter, deader, more shadeless words.

All such phonological hypothesizing as Edith was wont to supply is not without interest, but her reiteration of the value of her experimentations with prosody is really irrelevant to the quality of her poetry in *Facade.* Knowledge must oft precede appreciation, but a poet cannot tell a reader what he should experience and why. An individual experiences art best in his own way.

Edith's profuse and erudite explanations of the aural techniques and technicalities contribute little to the average person's enjoyment of her poetry. Cecil Beaton, for one, admitted that Edith's explanations were wasted on him. That he lacked a poetic sensibility, he readily admitted; and though he loved to hear Edith recite her lines and to read the words of poets she most admired, he remained insensitive to much of what he heard. As Beaton himself once said, Edith "could make any rubbish sound like poetry."[7]

Those less than enthusiastic about *Facade* maintained that the work had a measure of success mainly because of Edith's personality and showmanship. To rebut such adverse opinions was undoubtedly the reason Edith emphasized the technical aspects and musical cadences of her verse. But the question remained in the minds of many: was she a great poet or merely a talented charlatan? Over the next forty years of her life—in volume after volume of verse—she attempted to prove that she was a gifted author, a great poet worthy to reign in England's literary pantheon.

Chapter Four

Creditable Achievements

The Most Precocious

Sacheverell's first book, *The People's Palace*—a slight work made up of but fourteen poems—was published during the summer of 1918. A few of the poems had originally appeared in *Wheels,* but most were completed expressly for this collection. The youngest of the Sitwells, Sacheverell, who was only twenty at the time, was the last of the trio to be published. Edith was twenty-eight when her first work, *The Mother and Other Poems,* was published in 1915. Osbert was twenty-seven when his first collection of poems, *Argonaut and Juggernaut,* was published in 1919. In publishing *The People's Palace,* Sacheverell had the example and encouragement of his older sister and brother; but, as they readily admitted, he was the most precocious member of the family.

When still in his teens, Sacheverell had carried on extensive correspondence with some of the foremost intellectuals, artists, and musicians of the period. He is the only Etonian known to have exchanged letters with Filippo Marinetti; for the futurist artist and other avant-garde figures to have taken the time to answer Sacheverell's letters is proof of their high regard for his budding intellect. Then, too, at Eton Sacheverell read extensively about all the arts. "With an intelligence already highly developed," Osbert wrote of his brother, "he set himself . . . with an energy and intensity that were remarkable to amass knowledge—the sort of knowledge *he* wanted to amass."[1]

Edith and Osbert, justifiably proud of their younger brother, were disappointed that his first book attracted little attention. *The People's Palace* went virtually unnoticed. First, the war was still raging, and even literary critics who had escaped military service were concerned with the larger hopes of an armistice. Additionally, Sacheverell, apart from his contributions to *Wheels,* was an unknown, and the Sitwell name did not then command much attention. Finally, there was little about *The People's Palace* to attract either critics or readers.

Aldous Huxley was an exception. He admired *The People's Palace* and dubbed its author *le Rimbaud de nos jours*.[2] Edith went even further. She was convinced that a young poet—"one of the greatest that our race has produced in the last hundred and fifty years," as she put it[3]—had come upon the scene; and she saw no reason why a blood relationship should be an obstacle to her proclaiming the good news. Nor did Osbert refrain from singing the praises of his younger brother.

One brother, Osbert admitted, should not ordinarily proclaim another brother's genius, but he could not help wishing that he had been endowed with a hundredth part of his brother's creative power and sensibility. "I proclaim for him," Osbert wrote glowingly of Sacheverell, "a prodigious vigour of thought, of imagery and rhyme . . . an ability to produce a sense of prodigality and profusion . . . a boldness and largeness that set him apart from most of his contemporaries."[4]

While it is true that Osbert's, Edith's, and Huxley's views of *The People's Palace* border on hyperbole, one or two of the poems in the collection are not without interest, specifically "Pindar" and "Barrel Organs." In "Pindar," Sacheverell successfully re-created and combined the two legends of the acclaimed Greek poet: one, how when a babe asleep in the woods a swarm of honeybees settled on his lips; the other, how Pan stole Pindar's song and sung it on the montain tops. In "Barrel Organ," Sacheverell experimented boldly and forcefully with the syncopation of various sounds, especially the cold quick wind swirling and eddying about, arousing the poet's heart until his very nerves, "strung like banjo strings," began to twang.

In 1922, four years after the publication of *The People's Palace,* Sacheverell was ready with another collection of his poems. This second anthology he called *The Hundred and One Harlequins,* after a series of eleven poems he placed at the beginning of his volume. The title, let alone the poetry, perplexed some readers. Arnold Bennett for one found the collection "damnably difficult," That he could not make much of several poems disturbed him; still, he maintained that *The Hundred and One Harlequins* contained great beauty. Where, exactly, he was not sure: "You don't see it clearly. It tantalizes you. You see it moving dimly at the ends of misty glades."[5]

Sacheverell's Harlequins were not character sketches in the usual sense, as the title might lead one to believe, but rather vignettes of human existence enmeshed in the beauty of natural phenomenon. There were, furthermore, only eleven, not *one hundred and one* Harlequins. With those who wondered where the other ninety might be, Sacheverell was having a bit of fun. In Roman numerals eleven is written with an X and an I. If combined, X and I correspond to the Arabic number 10 and 1—101. Since the bromide about understanding preceding appreciation has much to recommmend it, the title was one way to dissuade less-than-perceptive readers from even bothering to read his poetry.

Those who failed to catch the significance of the title still recognized that several of Sacheverell's poems had much in common with Edith's and Osbert's *Twentieth Century Harlequinade;* and this troubled such readers. Sacheverell's poetry was often as incomprehensible as that of his brother and sister. A few marveled at Sacheverell's creativity and the fact that, whether from instinct or design, he allowed his unconscious to lead him whence it would.

As though to prove that the poet dreams while awake, Sacheverell apparently composed most of his Harlequins through a kind of reverie process that trusted more to association than to logic. Not only were many of his lines virtually impossible to decipher, to follow step by step, but his real talent, one critic proposed, had been obscured "by his occupation with theories . . . by the experimental temper of his age. . . . "[6] Like both Edith and Osbert, Sacheverell continually experimented. He was still a young poet and not entirely certain of his poetic voice. Accordingly, some of the poems in *The Hundred and One Harlequins* are partly in meter, partly in vers libre. Many are fragmentary in narrative and loose in verse form.

One critic labeled Sacheverell "cubistic." Not knowing quite what to make of the Harlequins, this critic nonetheless did not seem to mind that they "gambol . . . with unicorns, giants, phoenixes and lions," that several poems concerned "glass chariots and five league boots." A reader might be tempted to find in the verse more meaning that it holds, he feared, though one might also perceive "less meaning in the bizarre lines than is actually there."[7]

Catch a Falling Star

The Hundred and One Harlequins contains one poem upon which Sacheverell expended considerable time—*Dr. Donne and Gargantua,* which he had previously published in 1921 in a limited edition of 101 copies. A poem of almost 400 lines, he hoped it would ultimately become his *magnum opus;* for he added a second canto in 1923, a third in 1926, and three more in 1930.

The prime influence on all six cantos of *Dr. Donne and Gargantua* was Sacheverell's reading of Nietzsche. From the philosopher-poet, he borrowed several key concepts. Foremost among them is one that Nietzsche had used to advantage in *Thus Spoke Zarathustra,* namely an imaginary hero delivering long speeches to imaginary audiences. Another is the use of a hero or mouthpiece to represent a dominant idea. Influenced so by Nietzsche, it almost seems that Sacheverell was more intent in wrestling with profound philosophical questions of life, existence, sin, punishment, and death than in creating a genuine work of poetry.

That Sacheverell used for his dominant theme in *Dr. Donne and Gargantua* the futility of all human efforts to be like God would be obvious to one familiar with Nietzsche's philosophy. God, as the author of all life, is of course responsible for the existence of both title characters, Donne being an impersonation of intellectual and spiritual ambition, while Gargantua is the embodiment of the flesh and materialistic success.

Donne's familiar words, "Run and catch a falling star, / Get with child a mandrake root," serve as epigraph to the first canto. The opening lines portend a contest between the spiritual and the physical, between good and evil. Donne and Gargantua are the antagonists, and each is in competition with God, who does not directly interfere in the action.

In pursuit of their goals, "they set out from the Alps," make their way "down the mountain side," to "go forth as eagles." They ponder maps and plot their way. Gargantua soon reveals his vexatious nature. He rationalizes that God will not interfere with his malaciousness, and possibly the almighty may not even demand retribution. Only when the anthropomorphic God sleeps does Gargantua exercise his stratagems. When the almighty awakens, he learns that Gargantua had tried to usurp his place and has even founded a religion.

In the second canto, the narrative picks up at Rabelais's Abbey at Thelma. Gargantua is now preaching his new religion. To all who follow him, he promises an immortal existence. In laborious detail he relates to Knights and Ladies the dichotomy between himself and Dr. Donne. At the end of the canto, he affirms his intention of searching for the magical root: "Where is the mandrake? Like the meteor, lost./The silver cord is loosed. The golden bowl, broken."

Each of the four cantos that follows complicates the narrative further, but neither Donne nor Gargantua, nor their long speeches, enthrall the reader. In truth, *Dr. Donne and Gargantua* is a disappointment. First, it rambles on much too long; secondly, it fails to arrive at a reasonable conclusion. If Sacheverell's intention was to have the reader speculate upon God's intentions with the world, then he accomplished that end. Most readers would undoubtedly prefer some more logical conclusion and not be left wondering if God were only playing a game with Donne and Gargantua—very much like the kind of game that Sacheverell appears to be playing with his readers.

A strange admixture of drama, satire, and philosophical speculation, *Dr. Donne and Gargantua* is, at best, only occasionally successful. The conflicts as particularized in the figures of Donne and Gargantua one critic labels "fascinating," but even he laments that much of what Sacheverell has written fails to engage the reader; for the poem is "too overburdened with luxurious images and slightly self-indulgent longings." Even the most serious reader would find it difficult to refute this critic's final judgment that the work is "lacking in incisiveness."[8] Like many another extralong poem, *Dr. Donne and Gargantua,* despite a strong and imaginative beginning, tends to weaken and dissipate its strength the more it runs on.

Lyricism and Fiction

In the same year that Sacheverell published *The Hundred and One Harlequins,* Osbert was preparing another collection of poetry. Having made a name for himself as a satirist and literary critic, he now turned his attention to more traditional lyricism. In 1923 he published *Out of the Flame,* a volume of fewer than 100 pages. What the work lacked in size, it made up for in intensity. Osbert had tried to avoid the strident manner of his earlier verse—and, in the main, succeeded. No longer could he be dismissed as a satirical versifier or anecdotal abstractionist.

Out of the Flame consists of two parts. The first part contains poems that took their inspiration from moods wherein Osbert contemplated an ideal world of beauty and creative energy. By way of contrast, the second part gibes at the dull, cruel world of the proud, the privileged, and the powerful. Several poems in the collection come close to being witty, mildly amusing, and almost deft in their approximations, though none are especially memorable.

Richard Aldington thought otherwise. He was enthusiastic about Osbert's latest poetry collection. "The succession of clear, bright images . . . the poet's intense love of beauty, vivid imagination, hatred of cant and stupidity," he effused, "make *Out of the Flame* one of the most stimulating books of poetry which have appeared in England since the war."[9] Aldington had also written a generous review of Sacheverell's *Hundred and One Harlequins,* stressing in particular that as a poet Sacheverell knew exactly "what effect he wishes to make and how to obtain it."[10]

Having recently met the Sitwell brothers, Aldington acknowledged having "a slightly romantic feeling about them." Osbert, he added, "attracted me by his wit and honesty, and his brother by his passion for beautiful things and a sensitive taste which amounted to genius."[11] The Sitwells, it seemed to Aldington, were carrying on the tradition of the cultured English aristocrat. "They are the most effective evidence one can produce to readers outside this little island in support of the assertion . . . that imagination, daring, and wit still exist in our midst," he declared. "The three Sitwells make a compact and exotic oasis in the wide desert of contemporary British poetry."[12]

Pleased as they were to receive such gracious praise from a fellow poet, Edith, Osbert, and Sacheverell must have suspected that as a critic Aldington was guilty of what Matthew Arnold had labeled "the personal fallacy"; for other critics were far more subdued in their judgments of the Sitwells and their poetry. Acquaintances who regarded the trio as highly as did Aldington were judiciously cultivated. Anyone who failed to reverence their contributions to contemporary literature was immediately shunted aside. Aldous Huxley is a case at point. After being a close friend of the Sitwells for several years, he had the audacity to spoof Osbert and the whole family in one of his short stories.

In "The Tillotson Banquet," Huxley depicts Tillotson as an aged and neglected painter discovered by a young and ambitious critic. The critic persuades Lord Badgery, a wealthy art collector, to honor Tillotson at a banquet, during which everything goes badly. Huxley, in an attempt to be clever, modeled Lord Badgery after Osbert. He

made Badgery resemble Osbert down to the smallest details: "Behind
the heavy waxen mask of his face, ambushed behind the Hanoverian
nose, the little lustreless pig's eyes, the pale thick lips, there lurked
a small devil of happy malice that rocked with laughter."[13]

Badgery's erratic mode of conversation, as ridiculed by Huxley,
was imitative of Osbert's tendency to hold forth during serious
discussions. Badgery was an obvious physically and emotionally
repellent figure of fun. But Osbert was not amused. Nor were the
other members of the Sitwell family, for Huxley had also written:
"In the eighteenth century, the Badgerys began to venture forth
into civilized society. From boorish squires they blossomed into
grands seigneurs, patrons of the arts, virtuosi."[14]

The odds are that Huxley did not mean to wound the Sitwells
as deeply as he did. He simply could not resist deflating their egos
a bit, but what he wrote cut too close to the bone. To make sport
of his physical makeup was bad enough, Osbert thought; yet for
Huxley to mock everything Lord Badgery did and said was far worse.
Even more offensive was that Huxley had based the character of
Tillotson upon Henry Melvill, a senile actor who had been a matinee
idol during the nineties.

Osbert had met Melvill at Monte Carlo shortly after the war
ended. In 1921, when Osbert was visiting Lucca, an old Roman
city some forty miles west of Florence, he again encountered Melvill.
At the time, Osbert was traveling with Huxley and introduced him
to "Talking Harry Melvill," as the garrulous old actor was called.
Huxley never forgot the meeting, the amusing stories Osbert had
told him about Melvill, nor the interminable monologues he recited
about the London stage, Pater, Wilde, and other personalities from
the nineties that he had known. Melvill, Huxley concluded, was
too good a donnée not to use in a story.

When Osbert read "The Tillotson Banquet" he was not especially
concerned about Melvill—who was devastated when he learned of
Huxley's story. Neither was Osbert perturbed because he himself
had planned to use the colorful old actor in a story he would write
someday. Osbert was furious mainly because he felt Huxley had no
right to do a take-off on Melvill without first obtaining permission—not Melvill's, that is, but Osbert's.

Osbert pondered his revenge. He decided to retaliate in kind.
Though he had never written fiction, he would do as Huxley had
done and write a short story. Melvill would still be the focus, but

for Lord Badgery he would substitute a writer dubbed William Erasmus, an obvious stand-in for Huxley, at whom Osbert could direct some spleen. Erasmus, accordingly, is described as "tall and thin as a young giraffe, with the small head of some extinct animal . . . that subsisted on the nibbled tops of young palm trees in the oases."[15] To mock Huxley further Osbert wrote that Erasmus had become "more Italian than the Italians" after only a little more than a month in Italy, "even talking the language with such exquisite *bocca Romana* that the Romans were unable to grasp his meaning" (*TF*, 188).

Beyond such overt attacks upon Huxley were dozens of innuendoes that were unmistakingly aimed at Osbert's former friend. "The Machine Breaks Down," as Osbert entitled his story, was well received upon its publication in the *English Review* of December 1922. Not only did it prove an apt vehicle for getting the better of Huxley, but it was an excellently crafted work of fiction as well. Osbert, as it turned out, owed Huxley a debt of gratitude. Many years later Osbert wrote: "Indeed, it was only because of a friend of mine, a respected contemporary novelist, stole my stories, and because I resented the manner in which he twisted and spoiled them, and because I felt I could write them better myself, that I took to prose" (*L*, 59).

A Few More Stories

"The Machine Breaks Down" turned out so well that Osbert determined to try a few more short stories. His second attempt at a work of fiction, "Friendship's Due," was also a matter of literary revenge. An epigraph from Pope's *Essay on Criticism*—"Some have for wits, and then poets passed, / Turned critics next, and proved plain fools at last"—sets the tone and temper of the story. A poet, a critic, and a journalist are the lead characters. They are in the early years of what they hope will be promising careers and have banded together into a mutual admiration society.

Much of their time, when not occupied in praising one another, is spent in contemplation of suicide. Only after death, they feel, will their genius be fully recognized, while the more sudden and violent their end, the more effective for their posthumous glory. When least expected, the poet does shoot himself in a cheap hotel in Paris. The tragedy was not so much because of poverty, weariness, or ill-health, or the feeling that he was an unappreciated genius, as the recognition on the poet's part that he possessed so little real talent and that his reputation had grown out of proportion to it.

The critic, though he keeps promising to end his life as did the poet, fails to do so. Something may be due friendship, he rationalizes, but he must go on living; for, as Osbert caustically comments, "the critic's contribution to literature is, in reality, one of more importance than that of the creative mind, whether poets or prose writers—the shadow more lasting than the substance, the parasite more interesting and enduring than the victim on which it thrives" (*TF*, 73–74).

Osbert modeled the critic, Ferdinand H. McCullock, on a Belfast journalist named Louis McQuilland, who brought a measure of attention to himself when he denounced the Sitwells as founders of "The Asylum School of Poetry." Writing in the *Daily Express* of 22 July 1920, McQuilland complained that an appreciable number of Londoners were actually reading "the absurdities of Osbert, Sacheverell and Edith (that curious Chelsea trinity) . . . whose clever gibberish and clotted nonsense possessed scanty rhyme and no reason." Osbert never forgot McQuilland's attack upon him, his brother, and his sister.

A short time later, Osbert overheard, quite by accident, strange words spoken by the same Belfast journalist. "When I last heard him (I don't know him of course)," Osbert remarked in a letter to Grant Richards, "he was promising two elated ladies at a luncheon party in Fleet Street that he wouldn't, no, he couldn't really commit suicide."[16] And so McQuilland's bizarre conversation served as the basis of Osbert's entertaining story. In writing "Friendship's Due" he revenged himself upon the brash young journalist who had dared denigrate the Sitwells as belonging to "The Asylum School of Poetry."

Osbert's revenge theory of fiction worked so well in "The Machine Breaks Down" and "Friendship's Due" that he put it to good use again in a third story. In "Triple Fugue" he took to task Edward Marsh, the former editor of *Georgian Poetry*, mimicking him as Matthew Dean, "the type that, like certain Orientals, enjoys obscure power, loves power without the public appearance of it" (*TF*, 226). Marsh's physical makeup Osbert captured in malicious similes. The character Dean, has for example, "a nervous wriggling waggle . . . as if a ventriloquist's dummy is speaking—so thin is the wooden stalk of the neck moving in the too-wide socket of the collar bone" (*TF*, 223).

The plot of "Triple Fugue" gets underway with reference to the awarding of an annual Pecksniff Prize for English Literature and is marked by a variety of weird complications. To allow for a better perspective on the idolatries and stupidities inherent in the literary establishment of the twenties, the time of narration is pushed ahead to 1948. An undertone of sardonic humor manifests itself throughout the story and leads to three entirely different individuals killed in the crash of an airplane being assembled to form one revived composite person.

With "Triple Fugue," which is more than twice as long as "The Machine Breaks Down" and "Friendship's Due" taken together, Osbert had enough for a collection of fiction; but he completed three more stories in order to achieve a more substantial volume. To *Triple Fugue,* as he entitled his first book of fiction, he added "Low Tide," "His Ship Comes Home," and "The Greeting."

"Low Tide" and "His Ship Comes Home" are studies in senescence. Two old maids in "Low Tide" wage a heroic struggle to keep up appearances. In "His Ship Comes Home," an old lothario, heavily in debt from dandified living, believes his plight will change after he marries a wealthy widow, only to discover, much to his sorrow, that she is a shrew. "The Greeting" is a grim story in which a large green parrot, two years after witnessing the murder of it mistress, breaks a silence to reveal the name of the individual who crushed its owner's skull with a ferocious blow.

When *Triple Fugue* was published early in the summer of 1924, it attracted a good number of readers. There were those who admired its originality, its gallery of portraits that stuck in the memory. Some remained unappreciative of Osbert's deft satirical thrusts, not being able to connect Erasmus in "The Machine Breaks Down" with Huxley, the critic McCullock in "Friendship's Due" with McQuilland, or Matthew Dean in "Triple Fugue" with Edward March—despite Osbert's cleverly tipping his hand in the preface. "In humbly presenting the following tales of the Old and New Worlds," he wrote, "I should . . . wish to warn my readers that any character attempting to recognize himself will be immediately prosecuted for libel" (*TF,* 5). The preface may have served its purpose, for those Osbert had satirized in his unflattering portraits decided it was wiser to keep their peace.

Desmond MacCarthy, no admirer of the Sitwells from the beginning, acknowledged that there were "some very clever strokes in the portraits, some amusing distortions," but he decried the whole effect "as painful and strained." "Dingy Desmond" (as Edith referred to MacCarthy) adduced in his most precious style that Osbert's prose was "like wine which might be a vintage of delicate flavour, but it has been shaken up, and is full of bee's wings and cloudy deposits."[17]

A few other literary pundits shared MacCarthy's negative response to *Triple Fugue,* but the majority found more to praise than to censure. A critic in the *New York Times* extolled the six stories for their "stimulating literary flavor and quality one would like to meet with more often."[18] Each critic seemed to have his own favorite. "Triple Fugue," one maintained, was "much the best of the stories making up the volume."[19] "As a story," another asserted, " 'Low Tide' is the most successful."[20] Still another admired "Low Tide" but thought one other story its equal: "two of the six stories—'Low Tide' and 'The Greeting'—are works of genius," he wrote.[21] Such adulation accorded *Triple Fugue,* much to its author's satisfaction, was echoed by its many readers.

Osbert's reputation had received a tremendous boost. His excursion into fiction demonstrated that he was a worthy successor to such clever and subtle writers as Wilde, Beerbohm, and Shaw. Osbert had proved that he was more than Edith's younger brother. Through his poetry, his criticism, and now his fiction, he had established himself as a writer of some importance, one with a promising future before him.

Chapter Five

Ambitious Years

A Fairy Tale

During the same period in 1924 that Osbert was working on *Triple Fugue,* Edith was completing *The Sleeping Beauty,* her most ambitious poem to date. A work of over 1,500 lines, it makes use of the traditional fairy tale up to the point where the Prince approaches the sleeping Princess. Unlike the familiar Perrault version, however, at the end of Edith's poem the Princess is allowed to sleep on undisturbed in her own world.

Like virtually all of Edith's previous poems, *The Sleeping Beauty* contains several passages that are difficult to follow. Indeed, at first reading the narrative often seems opaque. Upon a second or third reading disparate elements coalesce to suggest a range of meaning. Indirection being the way of the poet, Edith's treatment of the story often has to be discerned from subtle use of imagery, rhythm, and meter. Carefree one moment and melancholy the next, the tale is moreover so embellished with a wealth of interlude and detail that it always seems vague and remote; but, then, maybe a fairy tale should be indefinite and illusive.

There is no mistaking the main theme: time's heavy hand brings folly and unhappiness more often than it does wisdom and joy. Dream aspects deal with the subjection of a youthful vision, personified by the Princess, to the necessities of age and its accompanying malice in the figure of the evil fairy Laidronette. Individual dream associations sprinkled liberally throughout the poem are meant to imply the mortality of pristine beauty is something to be mourned. In our mature years the world has "the same bright coloured clarity as those afternoons of our childhood," Edith once commented, but it is not the same. "The snow lies on our heart. Here we have a winter world, stripped bare of all its suckling leaves and the soul is face to face with reality."[1]

During the writing of *The Sleeping Beauty* it is obvious that Edith

47

was engaged upon an imaginative quest to recover the lost haven of her own childhood. Consider the telling lines:

> When we were young, how beautiful life seemed!
> The boundless bright horizons that we dreamed.
>
> And the immortal music of the Day and Night
> Leaving the echo of their wonder and their might.

The poem is structured in twenty-six cantos, containing from twenty to more than sixty lines. In addition to serving as prologue and an epilogue, the first and last cantos frame the narrative. In each, an old gardener speaks.

In canto 1, the scene is set at a dark house shadowed by the boughs of ancient trees. After playing his bagpipe, whose "music swoons with a safe sound," the gardener lays his instrument aside and says

> Keep . . . to the good safe ground!
> For once, long since, there was a felon
> With guineas gold as the seeds of a melon,
> And he would sail for a far strand
> To seek a waking, clearer land—
> A land whose name is only heard
> In the strange singing of a bird.

Continuing on, the gardener implies the mysteries of the countryside, its superstitions, a place where folk songs and fairy tales flourish. A young child listens intently as the gardner drones on and at the same time gathers plums and figs. "Beneath those laden boughs," he tells the child, "Dreaming is endlessness, forgotten beauty lies." He then begins a tale of "Beauty's mournful christening."

An unbidden fay, Laidronette, Princess of Pagodas, grows envious when she learns that gifts have been bestowed upon a newborn princess. Before any wickedness can befall the child, she is whisked off to a land of snow. Later, after being weaned from milk of doves, she is taken back to the royal court. Ruling at court are a Queen and a Dowager Queen, modeled after the poet's own grandmother and great grandmother, as Edith recorded some forty years later in her autobiography. *The Sleeping Beauty,* Edith noted, was "largely about my life as a child and young girl" (*TC*, 62). She also identified several other lesser characters with various housemaids and country maids whom she had known during her early years. The cruel fairies and harsh old people who gather around the Princess when she is in her deep sleep represent individuals Edith grew to dislike as she grew older.

Vague and minor complications do not hinder the Princess from growing up, but a little more than halfway through the poem she pricks her finger on a fateful spindle. During her long sleep, two dark kings appear, travelers from afar, and sing of a fair lady. One of them, Soldan, recites one of the most beautiful songs in the entire poem:[2]

> When green as a river was the barley,
> Green as a river the rye,
> I waded deep and began to parlay
> With a youth whom I heard sigh.
> "I seek," said he, "a lovely lady,
> A nymph as bright as a queen,
> Like a tree that drips with pearls and her shady
> Locks of hair were seen;
> And all the rivers became her flocks
> Through their wool you cannot shear,
> Because of the love of her flowing locks."

The Princess sleeps on, dreaming of unfathomable matters and distant places. Toward the end of the poem, a huntsman comes upon the scene. Is he the Prince in disguise who will bring the Princess out of her sleep? He disappears as suddenly as he appeared, and the Princess remains forever locked in a deep, deep sleep. In the final canto the gardener abruptly brings the tale to a close with an oblique reference to Jonah, who had "four and twenty daughters/ As lovely as the thick-fleeced waters." His final bit of wisdom that ends the poem is "To . . . shun the wave,/Nor sigh for a strange land/And songs no heart can understand."

The verse alters rhythmically throughout the poem. There are rhyming couplets and quatrains, lines in blank verse, haunting lullabies, an aubade, and nocturnes. Phrases and rhymes are occasionally repeated and similar elements reappear in different settings. Certain images are also echoed more than a few times, as in Edith's comparison of girl's curls with cream or curds and of clouds with hanging chalets. Such repetitions are apparently meant to emphasize elements of color and style.

Undoubtedly even Osbert, to whom Edith dedicated *The Sleeping Beauty,* could not fathom certain iterations. Nor is it likely that he could appreciate all the ambiguities in the narrative. He was not unwilling, however, to allow his imagination free rein—something several critics refused to do. Richard Le Gallienne, for one, found little meaning or beauty in Edith's poem. "We have merely a spoiled child of the Muses," he objected, "behaving with words as some spoiled beauty poses and postures before her admirers." As far as he was concerned, *The Sleeping Beauty,* although steeped "in all forms of exotic and fantastic literature," had been written "in imitative decoration without design and without decorative result. . . . "[3]

Virtually echoing Le Gallienne, another critic, after readily admitting the difficulty he had following the story line, complained the poem lacked "design." What the work needed most, he recommended, were "marginal comments like those to *The Ancient Mariner.*"[4] A third dismissed *The Sleeping Beauty* as "silly . . . difficult to understand."[5] Babette Deutsch was not quite so negative in her review of the poem. She pointed out that *The Sleeping Beauty* possessed what every good poem needs: "magic . . . and lyricism, and color." As a sister poet she could not refrain from giving Edith a bit of advice. In the future, Edith should "cease to juggle her materials like the bright hard candles in a glass bottle, but use them rather like chosen jewels on just such a golden thread as this legend of the sleeping beauty"; and if she did, why then Edith might achieve "something rarer and finer than anything she has yet attempted."[6]

Regardless of what adverse critics said about *The Sleeping Beauty,* Cyril Connolly, then a student at Balliol, remained thoroughly enamoured of Edith's poetic tale. "*The Sleeping Beauty,*" he wrote to a close friend, "was one of the loveliest poems" he had ever read.[7] He admired Edith's work so much that he even managed to have himself invited to tea. After meeting Edith and her brothers in the flesh, Connolly's admiration moved on to veneration. To him, the Sitwells were consummate artists, social and aesthetic paragons. They had their faults, he realized, but they were still dazzling monuments on the literary scene. "They absolutely enhanced life for us during the Twenties," he once told John Pearson, "and had they not been there a whole area of art and life would have been missing."[8]

Connolly was but one of the Sitwells' admirers at Oxford. Among many others were such dandies and aesthetes as Evelyn Waugh, Peter Quennell, Kenneth Clark, and Harold Acton. These "Children of the Sun," as Martin Green labeled the talented Oxfordians devoted to Narcissus and Adonis, had so thoroughly enjoyed *Facade* at London's Aeolian Hall that the Sitwells became important influences on their lives. Sophisticated and daring, Edith, Osbert, and Sacheverell personified the modern movement. All that was new and worthwhile seemed to point in their direction and reach a culmination in their works. The "Children of the Sun" read the Sitwells, discussed their individual works—and even imitated their actions.[9]

Acton, for example, created a stir at Oxford when he began to recite lines from *The Sleeping Beauty* through a megaphone from the balcony of his rooms. *Facade* having made the megaphone a requisite instrument for aspiring young poets, Acton put his own to good use. He had a duty, so he maintained, to nurture the aesthetic sense of students passing below in Christ Chruch meadow. And Waugh was so taken up with Acton's declamations that in the first chapter of *Brideshead Revisited* he has that aesthete par excellence Anthony Blanche duplicate Acton's performance and recite poetry through a megaphone—not Edith's *Sleeping Beauty,* ironically, but Eliot's *Waste Land*—for the edification of other Oxfordians.

Baroque and Baroquerie

About the same time that "The Children of the Sun" were reacting enthusiastically to Edith's *Sleeping Beauty* and Osbert's *Triple Fugue,* Sacheverell published his first prose work, *Southern Baroque Art.* To claim that Sacheverell's volume, which he completed when he was only twenty-two, set "a whole generation talking of baroque and rococo"[10] may be something of an exaggeration, but it is nonetheless true that all Sitwellians read it as a breviary. Unfortunately, there were not enough Sitwell devotees to make the book a best-seller. *Southern Baroque Art,* a succès d'estime, was critically acclaimed a most valuable contribution to the history of art.

In its own way, *Southern Baroque Art* complements Edith's poetry and Osbert's fiction. "The Sitwells," Kenneth Clark commented, "were using the baroque to express something of their own slightly frivolous, un-English attitude to life."[11] Sacheverell's study has dimensions far beyond the personal, however. Cyril Connolly summed up the importance of *Southern Baroque Art* best, perhaps, when he labeled the volume "a milestone in the development of . . . modern sensibility."[12]

Foremost in his study Sacheverell asserted that the baroque period, after having so often been regarded with disdain and misunderstanding, deserved to be seen in a more favorable light. One of the objectives in writing *Southern Baroque Art,* as he stated in an introduction, was to affirm his belief that "there has been no age in history . . . not worth examination, and that in the particular period I have chosen there are qualities to be praised of which there is a total lack in our generation, for self-confidence and fluency are, surely, two qualities which no one could deny. . . ."[13]

Sacheverell, accordingly, focused on the painting, architecture, and music of Italy and Spain during the seventeenth and eighteenth centuries. Rediscovery, revaluation, and evocation being paramount goals, he would not seek to present a straightforward historical account of the subject. "My aim has been so thoroughly to soak myself in the emanation of the period," he wrote, "that I can produce . . . the spirit and atmosphere of the time and place, without exposing too much of the creaking joints of the machinery, the iron screws and pins of which are the birth dates and death dates of the figures discussed" (*S,* 10). Since he was dealing with so many relatively unknown figures prominent during the baroque period, in an appended biographical index he took care of "the iron screws and pins," the birth dates and death dates and other salient details in the lives of various painters, musicians, architects, and political figures mentioned in the course of his book.

Nowhere in his study, however, does Sacheverell explain why the baroque developed in Europe about 1550 and why it flourished for some 200 years; why its art and architecture were typified by elaborate and ornate scrolls, curves, and other symmetrical ornamentation; why its music was marked by chromaticism, strict forms, and elaborate ornamentation. Nor does he mention, as a popularizer of this rather flamboyant style of art and music undoubtedly would have done, that the founder of the baroque was the Italian artist Frederigo Barocci, after whom the period was named. Having little interest in etymology, he also preferred not to deliberate upon the supposition that the term *baroque* may have originally derived from the Portuguese *barroco,* meaning *irregular.*

Sacheverell, apparently, had read everything ever written about the subject, as a glance at his bibliography makes obvious. Although he supplies the titles of almost fifty volumes, several of which were written in Italian, Spanish, and German, he apologized for not working up a more complete list of all the works he had consulted. "I give only the few most important modern authorities," he notes, "and those books of the seventeenth and eighteenth centuries most likely to interest students of the period under discussion" (*S,* 315).

Southern Baroque Art is an obvious consequence of all that its author had read and thought about the subject. It was as though he had inhaled so long and deeply that an exhalation became a necessity. To his credit, he kept the book free from pedantry and encumbering theories. An excellent example of interpretative criticism, it is directed toward the proper end of all art criticism: the fullest and most intelligent response to works of beauty. The volume is composed, moreover, as a work of baroque art, by being heavily ornamented with bits and pieces of baroquerie.

The texture of *Southern Baroque Art* is so elaborate, so full of exotic people and places, sumptuous occasions and customs, that at first plunge a reader might feel somewhat bewildered. Then, too, since so much of the subject matter is essentially novel, Sacheverell's quick transitions from historical fact to conjecture and his rapid transpositions of one art into terms of another, may easily overcome even the most serious reader. Such of course was not his intention; rather, he tried to evoke the atmosphere of the baroque, not by producing a critical survey, but by actually presenting in literary form the impressions originally proposed by the artists themselves. Occasionally, it must be admitted, his approach was a bit heavy-handed, his prose ornate. Occasionally he lost control of various themes and became too allusive in his symbolism and extreme in his judgments.

Had Sacheverell not had actual contact with so much that he covers in *Southern Baroque Art,* the volume would unquestionably lack much of the enthusiasm the work conveys. When Sacheverell was in his early teens, his father exposed him to the beauties of the baroque during family trips to Italy. Later, in his early twenties, in the company of Osbert, Sacheverell revisited most of the places that had moved him as a boy. And then, also with Osbert, Sacheverell took in the artistic wonders of Spain about which he had appreciatively read. Reading about works of art had its great pleasures, but to stand before actual paintings of Francesco Solimena in Naples, to gaze upon edifices designed by José Churriguerra in Salamanca, or to enjoy the magnificent canvases of Domenico Theotocopuli in Toledo was to experience beauty at firsthand.

A taste-maker, Sacheverell was the first critic to deal with several painters and architects generally overlooked in England. His evaluations of certain Neapolitan, Sicilian, and Salamancan artists brought them to the attention of devotees of great art. Today, for example, Domingo Theotocopuli (or El Greco, as he is better known) is widely recognized and highly admired, but in the 1920s he was virtually unknown outside of Spain; and, if known, hardly appreciated.

Sacheverell also focused on certain towns and cities in Italy and Spain that have become points of interest. He wrote, for example, of Catania, a seaport village on the slopes of Etna famed for its good food, ornate churches, and ducal palaces. Lecce, Copertino, Sternatia, and Nardo are just a few of the Apulian towns in which Sacheverell discovered prime models of baroque architecture. "It can never be stressed too much that in this part of Italy, some two hundred and fifty miles from Naples," he wrote, "you are, as it were, in another country from Naples or from Rome. It is as different as Portugal is from Spain" (*S*, 302).

At the same time, *Southern Baroque Art* was quite different from the few other studies of the period. Not one comes close to what Sacheverell achieved in his brilliant discourse. When comparisons were sought after, it was generally agreed that what Pater had done for the glories of the Renaissance, Sacheverell had accomplished for the baroque. As one critic put it: "No work of creative interpretation . . . written in English since Walter Pater's *Renaissance* . . . is more clearly marked with the stamp of original power and vital permanence."[14]

Ambiguity of Intentions

The success that Sacheverell's first book of prose had was, unfortunately, not shared by his next volume of poetry. In 1924, the same year in which he published *Southern Baroque Art,* Grant Richards released Sacheverell's *The Thirteenth Caesar*. Several critics justly complained about the length and monotony of this work. "Read here and there in a magazine Mr. Sitwell's verses have a bizarre interest," a reviewer for the *Saturday Review* wrote, "but when one is confronted by 112 pages of verbal contortions with such economy of idea, of emotion, of philosophy . . . one feels hurt by the dullness so unkindly thrust upon us."[15] *The Thirteenth Caesar* is not entirely without merit, though its ambiguity of intention and opulence of method do tend to obscure meaning.

There is no doubt about Sacheverell's attitude toward human existence in *The Thirteenth Caesar,* or his contempt for the ways of the modern world. The title of his work implies his scorn. "Caesar" is symbolic, not historical, and signifies the autocrat. "Thirteenth" connotes misfortune, "For ever since Democracy was born among us . . . /As people get more numerous, what's left grows smaller." In a staccato free verse, Sacheverell continues to hit at the grossness of the populace.

About the best that can be said for *The Thirteenth Caesar* is that it was experimental in design and limited in execution. Its queer mixture of flow and intricateness simply did not work in the way he had hoped. But Sacheverell could at least take comfort from the fact that adverse remarks leveled against *The Thirteenth Caesar* seemed as whispers drowned out by the roars of approbation accorded *Southern Baroque Art.*

Edith was of course delighted with the critical acclaim lavished on *Southern Baroque Art,* but she could not understand why *The Thirteenth Caesar* had not received the same reception. Osbert, on the other hand, clearly recognized the superiority of *Southern Baroque Art.* Edith had not actually journeyed to such out-of-the-way places as Catania and Lecce; Osbert had. Like Sacheverell, Osbert had also been moved to write of southern Italy and Spain, and he could fully appreciate how brilliantly his younger brother had done so. The journal that records Osbert's itinerary, which was published in 1925, he entitled *Discursions on Travel, Art and Life.*

In a few ways, Osbert's *Discursions* parallels Sacheverell's *Southern Baroque Art,* though it did not receive the same praise tendered Sacheverell's study. Nor did it deserve to, being mainly a collection of Osbert's rather rambling reflections on his visit to the heel of Italy, Sicily, and southern Germany. Most of what he had to say about the art and architecture of the places he had critically experienced is not without interest, but *Discursions* is more in the guidebook tradition.

As Osbert himself noted in his preface, the volume was essentially in the genre of travel literature. He would be satisfied, accordingly, if what he had written communicated a modicum of pleasure to gentle readers, especially those who loved to travel or enjoyed learning about the world from books. Travel, he noted, enables the mind to voyage more easily than the body, to move backward and forward through time as well as in space: "At one moment the traveller is able to measure the dome of St. Peter's in Rome by that of St. Paul's in London, at another to contemplate the march of Roman Legions and compare it with that of the passing Fascisti."[16] One who is an actual or mental traveler can easily flit from Italy to Spain to Germany, from art to architecture to music; for "travel is like a drug that permeates the mind with an indefinite but unusual tinge, stimulating and releasing, imparting a greater significance than they possess to the things that interest and amuse us."[17]

The critics were about evenly divided over Osbert's *Discursions.* For each one who found something to praise, another found material that he felt should have been omitted. A few did a balancing act, unable to decide whether or not *Discursions* possessed genuine merit. One representative review grumbled that though *Discursions* could "fill up a pitilessly rainy day," it was nevertheless "too journalistic to count as worthwhile literature."[18]

Regardless of what critics had to say about *Discursions,* in a peripheral way it was an important book; for Osbert had dedicated it to Georgia Doble, an attractive Canadian from a prominent banking family, to whom he had been introduced early in 1924. Impressed with her charm, he invited her to take tea with him and Sacheverell. She had read several of their books and had especially enjoyed *Southern Baroque Art,* and told Sacheverell so. Sacheverell and Georgia soon discovered they had more in common than their love for the baroque, and after a short period of time they decided to marry.

Much as they apparently liked Georgia Doble as a person, Sir George and Lady Ida, thinking no doubt about their own unhappy union, advised Sacheverell against the marriage. Edith did likewise; it was far better for a dedicated poet to remain single, she argued. Osbert, too, upset at the thought of losing the close support and friendship of his devoted younger brother, recommended that Sacheverell would be better off if he remained unattached. To escape such family bickering, Sacheverell and Georgia, who were very much in love, went off to France and, on 12 October 1925 were quietly married in Paris at the Anglican Church of St. George.

Melancholy Inclinations

In the same year that Sacheverell married and Osbert's *Discursions* was published, Edith released her *Troy Park*. Although she had completed the work in 1924, for reasons of her own she delayed its publication until March of the following year. She was now thirty-eight, still devoted to her poetry, but suffering from back pains and emotionally troubled by various matters, not the least of which was that the closeness she had felt to Osbert and Sacheverell was not what it had once been. In a letter she wrote to the poet John Freeman at the time, she lamented, "I was very gloomy about *Troy Park,* I don't know exactly why."[19] Her art brought her a measure of happiness, but her ultrasensitive nature began to incline her more and more toward melancholy.

A major collection of some twenty-five poems dealing with her youth, her family, and life in general, *Troy Park* takes its title from the home of her maternal grandmother in Wales, Troy House. Never having actually seen the place but hearing a great deal about it during her formative years had stimulated Edith's imagination. In her mind's eye she visualized Troy House, not as the seat of a large estate but as something remote and mysterious. The magical and wistful atmosphere of Troy House, as Edith imagined it, became intrinsic to most of the poems in *Troy Park.*

Among the autobiographical narratives in the collection is "Colonel Fantock," which she dedicated to Osbert and Sacheverell. The title character is modeled after a retired military man who served as tutor to Sacheverell and companion to Osbert. A delightful character, he is depicted as an "Old military ghost with mayfly whiskers / . . . blown by the cold wind" who could tell tales of "old apocryphal misfortune." The Colonel would often boast "of unseen victories / To a harsh unbelieving world. . . . "

Osbert, Sacheverell, and Edith are depicted in the poem as "Dagobert and Peregrine and I":

> . . . Dagobert and Peregrine and I
> Were children then; we walked like shy gazelles
> Among the music of the thin flower-bells.

And life held some promise,—never ask
Of what,—but life seemed less a stranger, then,
Than even after in this cold existence.
I always was a little outside life—
And so the things we touch could comfort me;
I loved the shy dreams we could hear and see—
For I was like one dead, like a small ghost,
A little cold air wandering and lost.

The children enjoyed the company of the Colonel, especially when

. . . he wandered over each old lie,
Changing the flowering hawthorne, full of bees,
Into the silver helm of Hercules,
For us defended Troy from the top stair
Outside the nursery, when the calm full moon
Was like the sound within the growth of trees.

But then one cruel day in June,

When pink flowers seemed a sweet Mozartian tune,
And Colonel Fantock pondered o'er a book,
A gay voice like a honeysuckle nook—
So sweet,—said, "It is Colonel Fantock's age
Which makes him babble."

Troubled by the remark about the Colonel's babbling, and concerned about his advanced age and nearness to death, Edith observed the poor old man's gaiety slowly give way to grief. Meditations upon mortality in the mind of a child follow; finally "On that June day/ Cold Death had taken his first citadel."

In "Colonel Fantock," as well as in such *Troy Park* poems as "The Child Who Saw Midas" and "The Pleasure Gardens," Edith delved into new depths of sensibility. In these three autobiographical works in particular she seemed most concerned about what she wanted to say, though she was not always sure about how much she was prepared to reveal. To a surprising degree, many lines in these three poems echo sadness and futility. Louis Untermeyer focused on this melancholic strain in *Troy Park*. "Miss Sitwell's increase in communication of the emotions has not dulled her imaginative vigor," he commented. "Her pages sparkle with observations that are both fantastic and exact. No one . . . . can surpass her verbal effects when she strikes the macabre note."[20]

In her next volume of poetry Edith continued to strike the macabre note. *Elegy on Dead Fashion,* published in 1926, is a poem of more than 100 quatrains that makes use of dozens of mythological figures from Jupiter and Juno to Chloe and Damon, to Eupheme, Phaola, Ambrosia, and Eudora. Pagan divinities are elegized and contrasted with Victorian women who are so interested in current fashions that they fail to realize that what they look upon as fashionable will someday be "grown dead and rotten." Victorian with their "deep black velvet bonnets," their "round straw hats deep-brimmed," and their "straw-coloured crinolines of faille," they are symbolic of "the anguished cold, / The crumbling years, the fear of growing old." "Still ladies in their carriages" drive the mountain to the gardens of the town. "Rich as a tomb" each one is dressed, but

> They are so poor they seem to have put by
> The outworn fashion of the flesh! They lie
> Naked and bare in their mortality
> Waiting for Death to warm them, childishly. . . .
> Come not, O solemn and revengeful Dead,—
> Most loving Dead, from your eternal bed
> To meet this living ghost, lest you should keep
> Some memory of what I was, and weep.

Elegy on Dead Fashion, published in a limited edition of 500 copies, attracted little attention. Critics avoided it. The few who reviewed it had little to say about some of the poems' haunting passages and flashes of beauty; they preferred to object that the poem lacked a logical structure, that it failed to crystalize events or emotions. A reviewer for the *Times Literary Supplement,* thinking no doubt of *Facade* and some of Edith's earlier poems, grumbled that she was "not wholly aware that her unicorns, fruits, and the like are . . . becoming clichés."[21]

Edith, deeply wounded by such trenchant remarks, began to harbor serious self-doubts. Fortunately, about the same time her latest effort was being either attacked or ignored, *Facade* was being enthusiastically received. On 27 April and again on 29 June 1926, public performances were given at the Chenil Galleries in Chelsea. "This time," William Walton is quoted as saying, "we finally seemed to have got it right."[22] There were none of the amateurish bunglings that accompanied the first public performance four years earlier at the Aeolian Hall. *Facade* had become a fashionable success.

The spotlight of glory was shining brightly on Edith, Osbert, and Sacheverell. They had written more than twenty volumes of poetry and prose. Each had had a few false starts, and had suffered at the hands of captious critics; but now they were recipients of critical and popular acclaim. No longer could they be denounced as supercilious aristocrats, egotistical clowns, or aesthetic revolutionaries. Each had written a work or two of indisputable excellence. Edith could glory in *Facade* and *The Sleeping Beauty,* Osbert in *The Triple Fugue,* and Sacheverell in *Southern Baroque Art.* And all three believed, moreover, that their best works were still to be written.

Chapter Six
On the Heights
A Masterstroke of Fiction

Having had more success with his fiction than with his poetry or criticism, Osbert carefully planned the writing of his first novel. When *Before the Bombardment,* as he entitled the work, was published late in 1926, it met with both critical acclaim and public acceptance. A masterstroke, *Before the Bombardment* was by far the best he had done.

The novel takes its title from the actual shelling of Scarborough in 1914 by German cruisers. In *Before the Bombardment,* the Scarborough of Osbert's youth becomes Newborough, a northern seaside resort just before World War I. A satirical comedy of manners, it portrays a moribund world of residential hotels and the social posturing that perished with the coming of the war. Tauntingly, Osbert focused on the prosperity of the upper middle class at a time when much of its wealth had been passed on to widows and spinster daughters, many of whom took to living in resort hotels. In Newborough (Scarborough) these lodginghouses were in earshot of industrial plants where "splintering steel rollers thudded at the town all day, and hammered, muffled by wind, all night long, as though secretly preparing it for a coffin. . . ."[1]

To alert the reader that *Before the Bombardment* was not an adventure story, a tale of derring-do, that precious little ordinarily happens at seaside resorts occupied by middle-aged women, early on in the novel Osbert wrote, "Our study must be told to the monotonous accompaniment of waves beating like drums of gathering armies: an accomplishment so tremendously out of scale that its very force adds, as it were, a certain main interest to the varying trivial and human events which the tale describes" (*B*, 66). What there is of plot centers on the truly trifling affairs of a bevy of selfish, gossiping old ladies.

Prominent among these superannuated characters are a Miss Waddington and a Mrs. Shrubfield. Social rivals, they do their utmost to cultivate a new arrival to Newborough, a Miss Collier-Floodgaye. A wealthy spinster, Miss Collier-Floodgaye is attended by a paid companion, Miss Bramley. They settle in for the winter at Newborough's Superb Hotel. Ever so slowly, Miss Collier-Floodgaye is admitted to the town's bazaars and other equally absurd social functions, at which all sorts of ridiculous things go wrong. The more insignificant the matter, the more is made of it among Newborough's socialites.

Miss Bramley, the salaried companion, had been schooled in her duties by a former employer, a martinet, but her present employer is not the usual bullying type of woman who demands that an employee keep to her station and be reminded continually of her place. From the outset, accordingly, the relationship between the paid companion and Miss Collier-Floodgaye is strained.

The employer, on her part, assumes that a paid companion can be a true friend. Her companion, however, cannot fathom the kindness of her employer. After all, Miss Bramley reasons, she was only a paid companion, and she expected to be treated like one, not to be given endless liberty in which she had nothing particular to do. She would not have minded "being bullied, being played with and tormented . . . "; for if certain codes were violated, if "the salaried graduate in the art of Friendship" were not properly treated, then a degradation would ensue, sufficient "to destroy entirely the paid companion's self-respect" (B, 257).

Osbert, having an obvious detestation for paid companionship, satirizes the relationship between Miss Collier-Floodgaye and Miss Bramley throughout the novel. Of all the occupations in the world that of salaried friend, he felt, was one of the most degrading. It was a declaration of spiritual bankruptcy, pernicious in its effect upon employer and employee: "For a poor woman to be forced to sell her friendship is infinitely more evil than for her to be obliged to sell her body" (B, 20).

The two women do their best to tolerate each other, at least for a time. When Miss Collier-Floodgaye grows mortally ill, however, Miss Bramley impedes her wishes in regard to a will. After the employer passes away, her will is located; but not having been signed, it has no legal standing. Miss Bramley is forced to realize that she cheated herself, for she soon learns that the unsigned will was made out in her favor. Miss Collier-Floodgaye's estate reverts to a distant cousin, who, thinking she is being generous, allows

Miss Bramley to choose one of her former employer's rings for a keepsake. At the end of the novel, Miss Bramley is left scanning the "Situations Vacant" columns. What may happen to her the reader does not really care; nor does he especially care, perhaps, about what may happen to the many other characters woven into the plot.

Before the Bombardment, it may rightfully be objected, has too many insignificant characters. Very much in the manner of Dickens, Osbert's favorite author, almost every chapter of *Before the Bombardment* weaves a few more pen-stroked individuals into the narrative. Obviously based on living models, they are not without interest in themselves; but, more often than not, they are extraneous to the story line. Then, too, Osbert elected to vivify them mainly through description than to develop them through dialogue or action. Even at the beginning of the novel, Osbert devoted almost forty pages to elaborate portraits of his dramatis personae. Arnold Bennett, for one, was not happy with such a method of characterization. Shortly after he read *Before the Bombardment* he recorded a tart observation about Osbert in his journal: "The man *describes* characters instead of showing them."[2]

Before the Bombardment's characters are, additionally, more often two-dimensional caricatures rather than three-dimensional human beings. The most important characters just about keep the plot moving along. They interact sufficiently with one another, and at the conclusion of the narrative all are symbolically disposed of. The grandee of Newborough, Miss Waddington, for example, is blown sky-high on the morning of the bombardment:

It was a dull morning in the first December of the Great War and Miss Waddington, then in her 87th year, was sitting propped up in bed at 8:30 before a creditable breakfast of tea, toast, poached eggs and marmalade. The local newspaper was by her side. . . . But . . . her attention was drawn away by the intruding cold dampness of the morning. . . . It was chilly, the old lady observed, distinctly chilly in spite of the fire, and she was just asking for an extra shawl . . . when, quite without warning, death darted at her from the sea, and Miss Waddington, and her bedroom with her, was pulverized, fading with a swift, raucous whistling and crashing into the murky air. (*B*, 310)

There is no denying that the novel is often heavy going, that the innuendoes of the portraits are too obvious, continuous, and occasionally stretched into dullness. "Osbert Sitwell lays his satire on with a trowel," John Lehmann once observed, "exaggerating the absurdities to the edge of burlesque and drawing out scenes long after he has made his point."[3] Now and then Osbert's satire crackles, but it is frequently perverse and at best only dryly amusing. Seldom, however, was he intentionally malicious.

Despite the complaint of one critic that since Osbert had spat on the whole Edwardian Age he should have entitled his novel *Great Expectorations,*[4] a careful reader perceives a sensitivity behind the novel's wit and satirical thrusts. As Roger Fulford has written, "Osbert parades his characters before us and we can almost hear the author's whispered comments as he draws our smile—*'pauvre humanité.'* "[5] In short, Osbert showed both sympathy and contempt for the victims of his satire, and it is this counterpointing that gives his novel a certain power to move the reader.

Although most critics were receptive to *Before the Bombardment,* several remained openly hostile. A reviewer for the *New York Times* objected that the novel with its thirty-six chapters was too long to sustain interest. "We wish Mr. Sitwell would take his book back and cut it down," he wrote. "We regret that the publishers did not have him do so before printing."[6] Osbert could ignore such reproving remarks, for every public attack seemed to have a private consolation.

After the novel's publication in London, to cite but one example, he learned that the Doran Company was going to publish the work in New York, and they wanted him to promote it in the states. To celebrate such good news he gave a going-away party at the Savoy. Among the seventy guests were such literary luminaries as H. G. Wells, Siegfried Sassoon, Edward Gosse, Augustine Birrell, and Arnold Bennett. The dinner was completely covered in the press. In addition to descriptions of a chrysanthemum salad served with a sumptuous meal, there were many flattering remarks by Osbert's guests about *Before the Bombardment.* Their judgments were undoubtedly influenced more by their admiration for Osbert the man than by their close reading of his novel. *Before the Bombardment* is a clever and diverting piece of fiction, but it is also an overextended, pretentious, dated novel ignored today by critics and readers alike.

In 1926, nonetheless, it did a great deal to popularize Osbert as a leading figure in contemporary literature. *All Summer in a Day* did likewise for Sacheverell in the same year. Osbert at thirty-four was widely heralded for his first novel. Sacheverell, who was only twenty-nine, was equally acclaimed for an autobiographical fantasia.

In his preface to *All Summer in a Day,* Sacheverell formulated his belief that it is "of more value to set forth your memories when you are twenty-five than after you have reached seventy-five."[7] Too young to write a conventional autobiography replete with facts, opinions, and appropriate anecdotes, he noted that he preferred to record only certain recollections from his early years and not do so in any systematic fashion: "I have chosen but one or two ghosts from my cupboard, brightly glittering ones by preference, whom I have dangled in the light for a few moments. . . ."[8]

Unlike *Southern Baroque Art,* his other prose work, *All Summer in a Day* was not written after much actual museum research and the reading of art books. Instead, in the writing of this book Sacheverell delved almost exclusively into his own memory in order to write of things no longer visible to the senses, to recall matters that once were "of flesh and blood, however cold they may be now."[9] To evoke youthful experiences, Sacheverell dwelt longingly on certain events and various individuals. In his mind's eye he recreated the Scarborough scene, its flowers and fruits. He delighted in remembering days of blackberrying across misty fields in North Derbyshire with his brother and sister, in recalling his admiration for an old tutor (the Colonel Fantock whom Edith wrote about in *Troy Park),* in recollecting long solitary walks taken during cold winters. He allowed himself to dilate upon aspects of oral and visual memory, to focus upon all he wished to treasure and to blot from his mind any unpleasant associations. How few, he observed, are the worthwhile ghosts of the past that we are able to linger over in our memories for even a moment. As valuable ghosts of our past slip further and further away, they tend to blur and disappear. What Sacheverell attempted to recall most vividly and record with accuracy he labeled his "autobiographical fantasia," and only as such should his *All Summer in a Day* be read.

Those who read his book in such a spirit praised it highly. "Subtly and . . . very beautifully expressed," a reviewer for the *Bookman* commented. "The descriptions are done all but exclusively in terms of emotional reactions, some of which will be tolerably familiar to all impressionable, imaginative people, while others possess a certain sharp individuality."[10] Those who approached the work expecting to read a conventional autobiography were obviously disappointed.

"Taken merely as a stunt in the fashion of Marcel Proust," a reviewer for the *Saturday Review of Literature* conceded, *"All Summer in a Day* is of course a clever piece of work." Still, he found Sacheverell's attitude "a little self-conscious, as if he were saying, 'See how much and how beautifully I can write about almost nothing.' "[11]

Even for those who may complain about a lack of substance in *All Summer in a Day,* the beauty of its prose possesses a charm all its own. Kenneth Clark believed that the book "contains some of the finest passages of prose written in our day."[12] Rebecca West was one of many others who seconded Clark's adulatory remark. "A delightful book," she wrote of *All Summer in a Day,* "and one that should shine in the public eye."[13] Sacheverell's autobiographical fantasia helped turn West into a Sitwell devotee. They were, she was convinced, among the few illuminants strong enough to light up postwar England. As writers, all three of the Sitwells were "the most glorious . . . that English life has ever produced. . . . They have done as much for culture in London . . . as anybody. . . ."[14] In the cause of culture, Sacheverell had also written a ballet, *The Triumphs of Neptune.* The work had been commissioned by Diaghilev shortly after his enjoying *Facade* during its 1926 performance. Diaghilev had been intending to produce an "English" ballet with spoken voices performed to music. Sacheverell proposed a balletic "English Pantomine' based on the characters found on Victorian "tuppence coloured" theatrical prints.

As a serious balletomane, Sacheverell had given considerable thought to such a scheme. Impressed by the young writer's original ideas, Diaghilev even accompanied him to Hoxton so they both could study prints in Pollock's Toy Theatre. Costumes were decided upon and other matters carefully planned. The chief characters were danced by Danilova, Sokolova, and Lifar; the music was written by Lord Berners. When *The Triumphs of Neptune* premiered at the Lyceum Theatre on 3 December 1926, it enjoyed an extraordinary success. The following month it was performed in Paris, where it also was enthusiastically received.

With the sound of applause ringing in his ears, Sacheverell believed it was time to stage a play that he and Osbert had written two years before during a visit with Max Beerbohm at Rapallo. Entitled *All at Sea,* the work was meant to be, as Osbert described it, "a satire on current silliness so near to that silliness itself that the silly would feel at home with it."[15] Basically, the play is a farce in which a number of smart society types move about between the cocktail bar and the saloon of a trans-Atlantic steamer.

Cecil Beaton did the scenery, and Osbert, Sacheverell, and Edith played the leading roles. The Sitwells were convinced they had a real hit on their hands, but the critics thought otherwise. *All at Sea* lasted a three-night run at the Arts Theatre Club. The Sitwells had come to personify wit, charm, brilliance, it was widely conceded, but those who attended the play agreed it was a dull and infantile piece of work.

Nor were the critics impressed with an extended essay, "A Few Days in an Author's Life," that Osbert published along with the play. Osbert, thinking himself another Shaw, found it incumbent, now that he was a playwright, to analyze the cause behind the decline of the British theater. After airing various artistic grievances, Osbert pointed out the superiority of the American theater and the greater insights of American critics. Little did Osbert suspect when he wrote his pretentious essay that English critics would point to *All at Sea* as a prime reason for the decline of the British theater.

About the same time that dramatic critics were panning *All at Sea,* Osbert published another volume of poetry, *England Reclaimed.* The pastoral poems that make up this collection are principally straightforward in narrative, as though Osbert were more interested in communicating exactly what he meant than in evoking emotional responses in the reader. He could hardly be accused of having an elliptical style, nor of employing peculiar linguistic originations, as Edith and Sacheverell had so frequently done.

Osbert's principal aim in *England Reclaimed* was to produce an uncomplicated kind of verse, poetry with discernible meaning that would transmit clearly if orally delivered. In an introduction to his volume he stressed such views. "It was to me as urgent a matter that a poem should be able to be read aloud with all possible effect," he emphasized, "as that it should look well on its printed page."[16] In *England Reclaimed,* Osbert did exactly what he had set out to do, but critics were unimpressed with the final result.

Obviously wounded by the critical response to *England Reclaimed,* Osbert still maintained the supreme "readability" of its poems. Sixteen years later he had an opportunity to prove his belief. On 8 April 1943, in Aeolian Hall, he read several of his eclogues from *England Reclaimed* to a select audience graced by the presence of the queen and two princesses. At the same gathering, Eliot read portions of *The Waste Land,* and Edith and Walter de la Mare read selections from their works. But Osbert, sitting next to the queen in the front row, felt that the "readability" of his *England Reclaimed* poems ruled the day.

Raising the Stakes

In the late twenties, the Sitwells were as prolific as they had ever been, but this did not work to their advantage; for critics seemed to demand that every work of theirs had to surpass what they had done before. The trio were not happy with demanding critics who continually raised the stakes. *Cyder Feast,* which Sacheverell published in 1926, is a case at point. Had this collection of poetry been written by any young poet other than Sacheverell, the Sitwells felt, it probably would have received better reviews. Instead, critics generally commented that they were amazed that a poet could write so expansively, as Sacheverell had, on flowers and fruit. Beauty blossomed on every page, they admitted, but they found his verse heavily burdened with an overripeness.

Sacheverell's next book, *German Baroque Art,* was better received. A sequel of sorts to *Southern Baroque Art,* it is a monograph on the art of central Europe under Leopold I and Charles VI. In writing the study, Sacheverell drew on the histories of the period to provide a backdrop for his descriptions of outstanding specimens of art in Germany, Austria, and Hungary. To round out the volume he covered the achievements of leading interior decorators, painters, and craftsmen in each country.

As he had done before with *Southern Baroque Art,* Sacheverell once more broke new ground. Nothing like *German Baroque Art* had ever been offered to English readers. No other writer had so adequately covered the history of the German side of the baroque manifestation. "The whole book is a model of artistic monograph," the *New Statesman* observed. "The writing is as good as need be, and there is no obtrusion of writing merely for writing's sake."[17]

Critics could not say the same about a slight volume of poetry, *Rustic Elegies,* that Edith published about the same time as Sacheverell published his *German Baroque Art.* Most of them found it undistinguished and unlikely to assist Edith's flamboyant reputation.

Mainly a collection of certain of Edith's poems that had already seen print, *Rustic Elegies* consists of "Elegy on Dead Fashion," which had been published the previous year; "The Hambone and the Heart," which incorporated sections of "The Mother" published twelve years before; and "Prelude to a Fairy Tale," which includes poems from *Facade* in a new framework based on mystical teaching of Rudolf Steiner, in whose teachings Edith was now interested.

As full as the poems making up *Rustic Elegies* are with wonderful passages and flashes of beauty, they contain too much artificiality and too many cloying nursery rhymes, too much criss-cross imagery and too many perverse juxtapositions. In straining after an exotic, esoteric style, she became at times less than intelligible. "Miss Sitwell dares you to understand her—and you do not," Mark Van Doren objected after reading *Rustic Elegies*. "She is hard to get at. When we do get at her we shall, I fear, merely be gettng at her limitations."[18]

Edith of course preferred to believe that she, Osbert, and Sacheverell had few limitations. Though she tried not to show it, she was perturbed by the poor reviews of her *Rustic Elegies*. Nor was she pleased with the mild reception Sacheverell's *Gothick North,* a two-volume study of medieval art and thought, received when it was published early in 1929. And she was troubled that Osbert's *The Man Who Lost Himself,* published about the same time as Sacheverell's *Gothick North,* was not as enthusiastically reviewed as his *Before the Bombardment* had been; that critics lamented that Osbert's second novel about a young writer who meets himself grown old and famous might have made a good short story, but that it should not have been attenuated into a long work of fiction.

A Radical Departure

Edith was now in her fortieth year, and the more she reflected upon her life and the sterility of all modern life, the more she wanted to voice such views in a major poem. That major poem, which she published in 1929, turned out to be her *Gold Coast Customs,* a work that William York Tindall labeled "Edith Sitwell's *Waste Land,* footnotes and all."[19] In several important ways, it resembles Eliot's *Waste Land,* but even more important is that her *Gold Coast Customs* marks a radical departure from *Facade, The Sleeping Beauty,* and *Troy Park.*

Poetry, Edith had come to believe, could be akin to moral wisdom. Her disdain for lofty moral themes had somehow vanished, possibly because of her admiration for Eliot's *Waste Land.* What fascinated her most about Eliot's poem was its didactic quality; so moved, she decided to play the role of a Sibyl. She, too, would denounce the spiritual bankruptcy of the time. Abandoning her dreamworld of sensuous mood and tonal patterns, her "pure poetry," she, like another Eliot, began to focus on the barbarism, the hypocrisy, and the misdirections of society.

One day early in 1928, while visiting the Ethnological Department of the British Museum, she hit upon the backdrop of her new poem. Fascinated by various African masks and shrunken heads on exhibition, she began to read studies of a culture she knew little about. In her notes to *Gold Coast Customs,* she acknowledged her debt to George Schweinfirth's *Heart of Africa,* G. F. Hegel's *Philosophy of History,* and several anthropological studies, especially those on tribal habits of the African Gold Coast.

From her reading, Edith learned that at one time in Ashanti the death of an important individual was followed by several days of ceremonies, during which the utmost licence prevailed and slaves were butchered so that the bones of the deceased might be washed with human blood. This custom gave Edith's poem its title and thrust. She set up an artfully sustained contrast between a tribe of cannibals and a Lady Bamburger, an English society matron filled with greed, lust, and kindred sins.

Like most of Edith's longer poems, *Gold Coast Customs* is deficient in plot. Though the work lacks a series of logically connected happenings, its more than 600 lines do have three main focal points: Ashanti tribal customs, a slum inhabited by paupers and prostitutes, and Lady Bamburger's social gatherings. The three points of focus, Edith indicated, are like tiers of a house: "The bottom tier is the negro swamp, which is a phantom, spiritual state, and on it the other two tiers—the terrible slum of the beggars, and the terrible slum of the cannibal are built. . . . "[20]

She effectively parallels the ferocity of primitive African rites with Lady Bamburger's parties; each, indeed, is indicative of the other; and, underscoring both, there is the overriding theme of personal betrayal and love disgraced. As the narrative advances, it becomes apparent that an African face mask is meant as a cover for the savage face of modern civilization.

In the opening stanzas, convulsive rhythms suggest a danse macabre. Every second syllable is stressed to imitate a drum beat. A rocking drum beat is further produced, as Edith herself explained, "by various flatnesses and depths of the 'a's,' the thickness and dullness of the 'u's,' and by the intertwining of words of different lengths. . . . "[21] In considerable detail she explained how various sounds also rise and fall, rock up and down, recoil and reverberate:

> One fantee wave
> Is grave and tall
> As brave Ashantee's
> Thick mud wall.
> Munza rattles his bones in the dust,
> Lurking in murk because he must.
>
> Striped black and white
> Is the squealing light;
> The dust brays white in the market-place,
> Dead powder spread on a black skull's face.

The lines that follow describe a scene of savage cruelty. In the ninth stanza a connection between Africa and England is established. King Munza of stanza 1, who belonged to a remote age, is set against Lady Bamburger, a twentieth-century aristocrat:

> . . . put your bones to bed!
> At lady Bamburger's parties each head,
> Grinning, knew it had left its bones
> In the mud with white skulls . . . only the grin
> Is left, strings of nerves, and the drum-taut skin.

In a tirade against the remorseless drift of contemporary philistine society, Edith, playing her role of an impassioned prophetess of gloom, states that

> . . . Lady Bamburger's Shrunken Head,
> Slum hovel, is full of the rat-eaten bones
> Of a fashionable god that lived not
> Ever, but still has bones to rot:
> A bloodless and an unborn thing
> That cannot wake, yet cannot sleep,
> That makes no sound, that cannot weep,
> That hears all, bears all cannot move—

> It is buried so deep like a shameful thing
> In that plague-spot heart, Death's last dust-heap.

Lady Bamburger is later merged with an Amazonian queen who grinds the bones of her own son's body for food:

> . . . the Amazon queen
> With a bone-black face
> Wears a mask with an ape-skin beard; she grinds
> Her male child's bones in a mortar, binds
> Him for food, and the people buy.

In an abrupt shift in focus, sailors disembarking their ships in the dockside slums are sought out by prostitutes:

> "Sally go
> Pick up a sailor.
> . . . why dilly and dally?"
> The dummies said when I was a girl.
> The rat deserts a room that is bare,
> But Want, a cruel rat gnawing there
> Ate to the heart, all else was gone,
> Nothing remained but Want alone.
> So now I'm a gay girl, a calico dummy,
> With nothing left alive but my feet
> That walk up and down in the Sailor's Street.

Sally's private misery is reflective of the desperate unhappiness of modern humanity. Edith demands to know why we do not

> Smell and see
> The sick smoke from London Burning,
> Gomorrah turning
> Like worms in the grave,
> The Bedlam daylight's murderous roar,
> Those pillars of fire the drunkard and the whore,
> Dirty souls boiled in cannibal cookshops to paper
> To make newspaper, flags?

Degraded beyond hope and doomed to wander the streets, Sally is one of the spiritual dead-in-life:

The heart of Sal
That once was a girl
And now is a calico thing to loll
Over the easy steps of the slum
Waiting for something dead to come.

From Rotten Alley and Booble Street,
The beggars crawl to starve near the meat
Of the reeling appalling cannibal mart,
And Lady Bamburger, smart Plague-cart.

Certain lines in *Gold Coast Customs* resulted from things Edith heard or witnessed. In a letter to Geoffrey Singleton she once disclosed that the line "The rat-eaten bones of a god that never lived" was a result of a frightful story of an illegal operation she learned about in her youth. The wind beating "on the heart of Sal," she added, came from seeing "a ragged creature . . . unspeakably famished looking . . . with a face that looked as if it had been ravaged . . . beating on an empty food tin with a bone."[22] Dozens of similar sights and sounds that had become lodged in her memory she put to good use in *Gold Coast Customs*.

Edith's effective use of sound in the poem can be heard not only in her tom-tom beats, which vary from the primitive rhythms of the jungle to the rhythms of modern jazz, but also in her echoing such decidedly unpleasant noises of groaning, bellowing, howling, roaring, squealing, whimpering, and whining. Intensifying the haunting aural quality of *Gold Coast Customs* is a repulsive imagery of flies, worms, rats, pigs, and weasels. The sights and sounds of the poem are such that, as Edith herself revealed, "it was written with anguish, and I would not willingly re-live that birth."[23]

At the end of the poem, everything is reduced to "primal mud." A Rich Man Judas, a Brother Cain, and Lady Bamburger are at one with the horrid superstitions and vile customs of the Gold Coast:

But yet if only one soul would whine
Rat-like from the lowest mud I should know
That somewhere in God's vast love it would shine.
But even the rat-whine has guttered low.

In a later edition of *Gold Coast Customs,* Edith gave the poem a new, less shocking ending. Convinced that there must be a greater design for humanity, she revised the above lines to read

> Yet the time will come
> To the heart's dark slum
> When the rich man's gold and the rich man's wheat
> Will grow in the street, that the starved may eat—
> And the sea of the rich will give up its dead—
> And the last blood and fire from my side will be shed.
> For the fires of God go marching on.

What Edith meant to imply with these revised lines, in which some expression of hope is obvious, she never explained. She made clear, however, that throughout *Gold Coast Customs* she tried to produce "not so much the record of a world . . . as its evocation."[24] She wanted her readers to take from her poem many thoughts, especially that they might cogitate "the rich man's gold and . . . wheat," "blood and fire," and "the fires of God . . . marching on." Such forceful imagery at the close of *Gold Coast Customs,* it is clear, intimates the sacred, a quest for belief, some metaphysical resolution to the enigma of life.

That *Gold Coast Customs* was Edith's most accomplished poem to date was the virtually unanimous view of critics. Kenneth Clark was deeply impressed by the emotional quality of the work; yet the poem disturbed him. "It leaves us in the chaos of despair, and art is the opposite of chaos," he complained.[25] A few reviewers focused on Edith's suffocating imagery, her prosodic diversions, and her occasional obscurity. Those truly stirred by the poem paid little attention to caviling critics. Yeats, for example, so admired *Gold Coast Customs* that he was moved to comment: "Something absent from all literature for a generation was back again, and in a form rare in the literature of all generations, passion ennobled by intensity, by endurance, by wisdom."[26]

Chapter Seven

Wellsprings of Creativity

A Prose Interlude

In March 1930, Faber and Faber published Edith's first important prose work, a biography of Alexander Pope. Two years before she had begun researching the life of that "small, unhappy, tortured creature, who is the greatest of our poets . . . and who is . . . perhaps the most flawless artist our race has produced."[1] She had several good reasons for doing a study of Pope.

Whatever effects *Gold Coast Customs* may have had on Edith's inner life, she reasoned that a work of prose would not be so emotionally draining as the writing of another serious poem. A change in pace seemed wise. She had no fears that the wellsprings of her creativity were drying up, for she still wrote poems on occasion. What she did not realize at the time was that she would not publish any poetry over the next ten years of her life.

During what proved to be a long and difficult period, she spent most of her energy not in thinking about Pope or poetry but in taking care of Helen Rootham. Ever loyal to her former governess, who had grown arbitrary and contentious because of a terminal illness, Edith cared for her in a Paris flat. "My life there," Edith later revealed, "was unmitigated hell" (*TC*, 158). She did not mind getting up at dawn; nor did she much mind the nursing and housework she did all day long; but she found it difficult and distracting to tolerate "the open accusations of wickedness and the threats . . ." (*TC*, 158).

Feeling obligated to her former governess, Edith assumed all financial responsibilities. And this is perhaps the chief reason Edith undertook a life of Pope, for Helen lingered in her illness until 1938. Seriously short of funds, Edith anticipated sufficient royalties from her study of Pope to care for her debts, but mixed reviews did little to move her book. A first edition of 4,000 copies had to be remaindered five years later. The days when the Sitwell name was a novelty were over, and Edith feared that a partial eclipse in her career had taken place.

The poet she had chosen to write about had also suffered almost a total eclipse early in the twentieth century. Matthew Arnold's strictures about Pope had gained academic respectability, and Oscar Wilde's quip about the two ways of disliking poetry—one, to have a complete aversion; the other, to like Pope's verse–had its epigrammatic force. Regardless of what Arnold, Wilde, and other critics had said, Edith still had a great admiration for Pope's poetry, and she even identified closely with his life and art. It is not difficult to understand why.

There were many similarities between them. Physically, they were antipodal in size, Pope being on the dwarfish side and Edith six feet tall; but they both had suffered a curvature of the spine. "Though he was deformed," Edith wrote, "people with beautiful shapes surrounded him, were proud of knowing him—if he did not make love to them. And only too soon he learned not to do that" (AP, 17). Pope, physically weak and ailing, must have had "strong and sensitive hands," Edith reasoned; "otherwise he would not have attained to the supreme mastery of texture and understanding of the accumulation of qualities to which his extraordinary variations is due" (AP, 266). Edith was as fascinated with Pope's hands as she was with her own, for she had taken to painting her long nails with a bright silver polish and to adorning her thin fingers with marble-sized rings.

Having a complete affinity with Pope's work, she maintained that it required an informed reader of some sensibility to respond fully to his art. A general blighting and withering of the poetic taste had taken place, however. There was a current misunderstanding of the aims and necessities of poetry. Most readers, she believed, had not recovered from the cold, damp mossiness that had tainted the public taste for some fifty or sixty years. To them, Pope appeared not a great poet, but a man deformed as much in spirit as in body.

Writing about the author of *The Rape of the Lock*, Edith realized would be difficult and dangerous, since whatever she wrote of its very nature would "injure personal susceptibilities and make evident the lack of sensibility towards poetry, of some of our more eminent bores" (AP, 1). Moreover, great writers—Pope and herself included—being individuals of genius, she felt could hardly escape vicious attacks in any age. As she wrote of Pope, while obviously thinking about herself: "The quarry is possessed of genius, and is therefore meant to be hunted and half-killed" (*AP*, 8).

Believing, furthermore, that a great poet of necessity had to have a superior character, she preferred to regard Pope as a good hearted, lovable, generous individual. While admitting difficulty in disentangling the evidence, she nevertheless ignored most of the unflattering stories about him. She could hardly deny his vanity, the rather devious stratagems he used to call attention to his works, and his contempt for critics; but her approach was mainly that of defense and vindication.

Behind his bitter tongue and malicious manner, Edith endeavored to prove, the "Wicked Wasp of Twickenham" was actually benign and personable, "his life's record . . . one of loyalty to friends, unchanging love where love was not betrayed, financial generosity, and . . . the most extraordinary delicacy and kindness" (*AP*, 11). That Pope could be formidable and terrible when aroused she did not deny. The point that so many biographers missed, she pointed out, was that Pope had to defend himself against "a thousand venemous little scribblers whose bodily powers were greater than his . . . ," but when attacked, he was able "to deliver harder blows . . . than the majority of his aggressors were able to administer to him" (*AP*, 11–12).

In eighteen chapters Edith concentrated on what she regarded as the five principal aspects of her subject's life: his early childhood, his friendships, his literary battles, his declining years, and his prosodic techniques. Of necessity, Edith had to rely heavily upon secondary sources. She was not academically trained, knew little about original research, and cared less about examining primary source material. Her approach was more that of eulogist than objective biographer.

One of the many critics who attacked Edith for her enthusiasms, for not treating Pope's life more objectively, was Geoffrey Grigson. Edith's study was filled with pretentious nonsense, he grieved, and he zeroed in on what he judged to be the volume's most glaring defects. "Miss Sitwell asks for it by her annoyance, her arrogance, her self-satisfaction, her superiority to mere critics and scholars," he complained. "It would be easy to pillory," he went on, "her ignorance of psychology . . . her parrot repetitions, her tricks of fine writing which cover absence of original research and shallowness of thought." Grigson was not even appreciative of the book's one real strength—its analysis of Pope's prosodic mastery.

In her discussion of Pope's poetry, Edith focused first on the subject in general and creativity in particular. "I believe," she noted, "that a poem begins in a poet's head, and then flows in his blood, as a rose grows among its leaves" (AP, 265). Then she moved on to Pope's use of the heroic couplet. Blank verse, she asserted, would have been impossible to a poet of Pope's tiny weak body, but "the stopped heroic couplet, with its sustaining rhymes . . . was born to be his measure" (AB, 266). Next she defended Pope's use of the closed couplet against charges of monotony. She cited specific examples of rhythm and texture to support her contention that only to an insensitive ear would a Popeian couplet be monotonous. Emphasizing the possibilities of infinitive variation within limited structure, she discussed in detail Pope's use of caesura, which he utilized skillfully not only to vary the music of his verse but also to heighten meaning. "We might as well complain," she concluded, "that the world is monotonous because it is round, and because it circles the sun, as complain about the monotony of Alexander Pope" (AP, 278).

Even in her tendentious examination of Pope's prosody, Edith, far from being dull, is provocative and stimulating. Mark Van Doren adjudged her study a novelty. Delighted to find her writing about Pope as if he were mysterious and wonderful, Van Doren rendered one of the most critically astute opinions of Edith's study of Pope. "As a biography," he wrote, "Miss Sitwell's book will hardly do. As eulogy it is delicious, and as criticism, even if it is extravagant, it takes its place among the necessary deeds to be done for the honor of Twickenham's angry swan."[3]

Although not entirely displeased by Van Doren's remarks, Edith was happy that her study helped initiate something of a Pope revival; but she was troubled that a multitude of poor reviews resulted in limited sales. The poor reception of *Alexander Pope* made her especially anxious about the reception of her *Collected Poems,* which was then being readied for publication. Over a period of some twenty years, her poetry had been praised and castigated, adulated and ridiculed. What impression would her poems make when published in a single volume? Would her limitations be more apparent?

Her fears proved unfounded. When her *Collected Poems* was published in June 1930, it was greeted with critical acclaim. As usual, there were detractors, but they represented a minority. The majority opinion held that few modern poets had made such a significant contribution to contemporary literature. Her poetry spoke for itself; it required no interpreters, no apologists, no publicists. Like another Alexander Pope, Edith had suffered for her art, had tolerated years of prejudice, but with the publiction of her *Collected Poems* it was obvious that she was as worthy of her laurels as Pope had been worthy of his some 200 years before.

A Continuing Love Affair

Edith's love for Pope's neoclassical poetry was equaled by Sacheverell's passion for the baroque, which he first made manifest in 1924 with *Southern Baroque Art* and again two years later with *German Baroque Art*. In 1931, he revealed his continuing affection for the subject when he published his *Spanish Baroque Art*. Once again, as he had in his two previous studies of the baroque, he covered the subject with infectious enthusiasm.

Few English readers knew much about the unique art of the Iberian Peninsula. The names of José Churriguerra and Pedro de Ribera were virtually unknown outside Spain before Sacheverell focused attention upon them. Nor did travelers to Portugal visit one of the most unusual ecclesiastical structures in the country— the magnificent chapel in the Lisbon church of Sao Roque built to design by Vanvitelli for Joao—before Sacheverell wrote glowingly about it in his *Spanish Baroque Art*.

As fascinating as *Spanish Baroque Art* is in its own fashion, however, there were few devotees of the subjects to guarantee the volume a wide sale. It found its readers mainly among those who had read and admired Sacheverell's two previous studies of the baroque, many of whom prided themselves on being amateur art historians. Additionally, travelers to Spain and Portugal put the study to good use. Although he had not planned *Spanish Baroque Art* to serve as a Baedeker,' it served such a purpose and can still be glimpsed in the hands of erudite tourists hunting down truly worthwhile things to see in Spain and Portugal.

Edith was of course delighted with Sacheverell's books on the baroque; in fact, his volumes of art history inclined her to try a volume of social history. She decided to do a study of Bath and its development under the uncrowned monarchy of Beau Nash. Images of what life might have been like when Nash and eighteenth-century gentility vacationed there filled her mind. The result is an evocation of the Augustan Bath and the lives of those individuals who enjoyed its splendors.

As a child, Edith had stayed at the famous watering place with her grandmother, and she had frequently visited the city as an adult. Since her study was to be essentially historical, she found no reason to visit Bath while doing her research. Her primary interest was not in the city itself but in chronicling the interplay of various aristocrats and eccentrics who had inhabited the place. Accordingly, she wrote most of *Bath* while staying in Paris with Helen Rootham. When time allowed, she read up on the subject from books that had been sent her from London libraries. Oftentimes she would force herself to write continuously for five or six hours a day.

Faber and Faber had commissioned *Bath* for publication in the spring of 1932. They were anxious for Edith to complete her manuscript on time, and she was just as eager to do so, since the chief reason for undertaking the work was the royalties she hoped it would earn. All 1,500 copies of *Bath* sold out quickly, and Faber and Faber requested that Edith do another prose study, this time one on eccentricity, a subject close to her heart. She went to work on her third book of prose immediately and within the year completed *English Eccentrics*—a biographical study of quacks, cranks, hermits, sportsmen, and dandies commemorated largely because of their private and public extravagances. The work was so well received that Edith considered adapting it for the stage. Fortunately, all plans came to naught; for had *English Eccentrics* been dramatized, Malcolm Williamson would not have composed the music, nor Geoffrey Dann written the libretto, for what turned out to be a successful opera when first performed in May 1964.

Despite the vast amount of time Edith had given to the reading, writing, and rewriting required for her to complete *English Eccentrics*, she still met on occasion with such literati as James Joyce, Ford Madox Ford, and Gertrude Stein, usually at Sylvia Beach's Shakespeare & Company Bookshop. Being part of the Parisian literary scene pleased her at first, since it allowed her respite from taking care of Helen Rootham and the strain of meeting publication deadlines. She enjoyed the company of other writers, but she piqued them about as often as they irritated her. Her chief enjoyment at the time, however, was musical, not literary. She loved to attend the Théâtre des Champ-Elysees to hear the music of her favorite composer, Beethoven. But like her taste in poetry, her taste in music fluctuated constantly. After she read Sacheverell's new book on Mozart, which he published early in 1932, she came to appreciate Mozart's genius and began to speak of him as frequently as she had of Beethoven—and often more glowingly.

The Music of Mozart

Sacheverell's interest in the art and architecture of Germany, which he had first expressed in *German Baroque Art*, led him to study their parallels in the music of Mozart. Being the author of the only book in English that dealt exclusively with the art and architecture of the Teutonic states in the eighteenth century, Sacheverell believed that he could successfully convey the atmosphere of Mozart's music. Far from lagging behind the other arts or merely reflecting them, music, he would demonstrate, is one of the first to embody cultural trends.

Any study of Mozart, Sacheverell reasoned, if it were to meet with success, had to appeal to several sorts of readers. Even those unfortunate few who cordially disliked music could not help being interested in Mozart merely as a phenomenon. Those who dismissed him as being mainly an affair of airs and graces, of tinkling melody and facile ornament, could become devotees of his music if it were presented in proper fashion. And there were the few who would want to learn more about the paradoxical virtuosity of Mozart's genius, those for whom everything he composed was sacred and beautiful. With such a broad audience in mind, Sacheverell began to delve deeply into the life of the greatest artist of the rococo age.

In the opening chapter of his study, which he entitled simply *Mozart*, Sacheverell covered the basic facts and anecdotes of the prodigy. He then discussed Mozart's rococo period (1771–81), and his Viennese period (1781–88). Before discoursing upon the last years (1788–91), Sacheverell devoted individual chapters to Mozart's chamber music, concertos, church music, and symphonies. In retelling the story of Mozart's life, Sacheverell focused upon the mental and emotional conditions out of which flowed so many remarkable musical works. Taking a clue from Edith's study of Pope, Sacheverell also concerned himself with the relationship between the composer's creativity and his physical makeup: "Mozart's music is always that of the small, delicate man.[4]

In chapter 12, "Some Little-Known Masterpieces," which serves as an epilogue, Sacheverell writes engagingly of Mozart's divertimenti, of his instrumental trios, and his works for the mechanical organ and glass harmonica. That being done, in his final paragraphs Sacheverell compared Mozart with Beethoven and Bach.

Beethoven, Sacheverell proposed, "reaches beyond Mozart, but it took years of heroical energy" (M, 181). Beethoven's genius, nevertheless, was not so adaptable as that of Mozart, for the former lacked the latter's interest in the timbre and particular properties of different instruments. Though Beethoven may have had more force than Mozart, he was deficient in poetry, in a sense of beauty. Mozart's range, furthermore, was greater; his sense of wonder superior. With his understanding of human character, Mozart "in his supreme moments floated easily where Beethoven climbed to with difficulty; he had elegance which Beethoven never possessed; and he pronounced with certainty, truths that Beethoven took, blindly, on assurance" (M, 182).

In Sacheverell's opinion, if Mozart be compared with Beethoven, there is no question of the former's greater subtlety of thought and higher natural equipment; but supremacy vanishes when Mozart is compared with Bach. Mozart was, more or less, an end in himself, having no posterity, while Bach stood between the past and the future, the summary of both. The fiber of Bach's thought was simply stronger than that of Mozart's. Sacheverell's final verdict: "Mozart had qualities which no other musician has ever had—except Bach" (M, 182).

In an attempt to amplify even further the musical genius of Bach and Mozart, Sacheverell alluded unfavorably to the rage for Wagner. Most serious music, Sacheverell ventured, was quite beautiful before Wagner, "whose loud . . . personality and unpleasant literary associations should have perished long ago" (M, 164). If such a slur were not enough, he went on to mention Wagner's "blatant vulgarities and his tweed-clad tunes" (M 169). Sacheverell had no desire to stir up controversy, but his discordant remarks about Wagner did just that.

Ernest Newman, one of the foremost English Wagnerians, led off. In his column in the *Sunday Times*, he dismissed Sacheverell's *Mozart* as strictly the work of an amateur: "Mr. Sitwell seems to be dimly aware that his view of Mozart is not that of . . . modern students of the master, but he brushed their conclusions aside with the airy remark that the critics have taken an all too serious point of view . . ."[5] Sacheverell's study, Newman pontificated, was a failure because of an insensibility to music and a limited perception of the subject. As for Sacheverell's adulation of Bach and Mozart and his indifference to Wagner, Newman wrote that if Sacheverell knew anything about music he would know that Wagner had a strong appeal to the finest musical minds. Perhaps it would be unreasonable, Newman concluded, to expect Sacheverell to have any worthwhile perceptions of Wagner—or, indeed, of Mozart.

Aggrieved by Newman's biting remarks, Sacheverell struck back. In a letter to the *Sunday Times* he retaliated by asking several pointed questions, one of which was if Newman had attacked his *Mozart* principally because the study failed to admire the composer of *Tanhäuser* and *Parsifal*.[6] In a follow-up column Newman decided to bait Sacheverell once again. With obvious joy he parried Sacheverell's questions right and left, and drove home with a final declaration: "Mr. Sitwell is either extremely simple or thoroughly ingenuous when he tries to make out that reasoned criticism . . . is on all fours with his own attitude toward Wagner . . ."[7]

Newman preferred not to let the matter drop and went after Sacheverell a third time.[8] Bolstered by Osbert, Sacheverell decided to respond once more to Newman's charges.[9] Concerned now that Edith might also enter the fray, that he would have to fend off all three Sitwells, Newman reasoned that it was wiser to back away. Possibly he had been too severe. After all, Sacheverell had actually let a bit of fresh air into the rather stuffy genre of musical criticism that Newman realized he himself often typified.

On his part, Sacheverell was forced to admit that he was very much the amateur that Newman had proclaimed him to be. Never one to take adverse criticism lightly, Sacheverell, instead of being discouraged, began to delve deeply into musicology. Then, more properly schooled, and using the same basic formula he had employed in the writing of *Mozart*, he went on to complete monographs of *Liszt* (1934) and *Scarlatti* (1935), as well as a tribute to Offenbach which he entitled *La Vie Parisienne* (1937).

The more he studied and wrote about Liszt, Scarlatti, and Offenbach, the more he came to admire their music; but his supreme favorites remained Mozart and Bach. Somehow he never felt up to doing a full-length study of Bach, yet one of Sacheverell's most sustained and imaginative passages of musical interpretation, found in his *Splendours and Miseries* (1934), is devoted to Bach's organ fugues.

Majestic works of Art

During the period that Sacheverell focused on music, art, and architecture, he tended to neglect his verse. As though to prove to himself that he still had the touch, he would occasionally pen a few poems. In 1933, he gathered these poems together and published them under the title *Canons of Giant Art: Twenty Torsos in Heroic Landscapes*.

These ambitious *Canons*, as their title indicates, glorify dedication, love, ritual, and heroism. Several take their origin from majestic works of art that Sacheverell admired. The third, "Aeneas Hunting Stags upon the Coast of Libya," is his poetic response to the painting by Claude in the Brussels's Museum; the fourth, "The Royal Hunt and Storm in the Forest," commemorates Queen Dido's adventure in Carthage as inspired by Berlioz's opera *Les Troyens*; the eleventh, "Landscape with the Giant Orion," is a reaction to the painting of Poussin in the Metropolitan Museum, New York; and the thirteenth, "The Hermes of Praxiteles," adulates all that the statue at Olympia embodies; while the fourteenth, "The Farnese Hercules," does the same for that statue at Naples.

All twenty of the *Canons* emphasize that the most valuable experience one can have in life are those related to painting, sculpture, and music. Like Yeats in his "Sailing to Byzantiums." Sacheverell implies that he prizes works of art more highly than the artists who brought such beauty into being. Unlike Eliot, who in *The Waste Land* wrote about fragments shored against ruins, Sacheverell dwelt longingly on fragments that lead a reader to a consideration of mythological civilizations that, in their diversity and grandeur, offer a provocative response to our disparate age.

Few critics may concur with Edith's opinion of the fifth poem, "Agamemnon's Tomb"—"one of the greatest poems written in the English language for over a century"[10]—but it is one of the best in the collection. "The poem stands out," wrote John Lehmann, "because in it, the poet, more than anywhere else in the *Canons* . . . appears deeply engaged with his subject."[11] Sacheverell's interest in the reputed tomb of Agamemnon was first touched off by his reading about Schliemann's discovery of the huge, bee-hive underground vault below the citadel at Mycenae, obviously the resting place of a great man. Schliemann conjectured that the body with the golden mask found in an inner chamber had to be that of Homer's great king.

When Sacheverell first stood in the royal tomb, thoughts of the inscrutability of death flooded his mind. Appropriately, the pace of his poem is dirgelike, the matter implacable, his phrases swelling and modulating in Mozartian splendor. Agamemnon is dead and residing in his tomb, but even in his death there is grandeur. Bees flit in and fill the cavity

> With the honey of the asphodel, the flower of death,
> Of thyme, rain sodden, and more sweet for that;
> Here was their honeycomb, high in the roof.
> I heard sweet summer from their drumming wings,
> Though it wept and rained and was the time of tears;
> They made low music, they murmured in the tomb.
> As droning nuns through all a shuttered noon,
> Who prayed in this place of death, and knew it not.

In a later year, Sacheverell revisited the tomb to ponder further the inexplicability of physical extinction. Can Agamemnon reveal the meaning of death?

> O happy Agamemnon, who was luckless, living,
> Happy in death, in the hollow haunted room,
> Your very name is the treading of a spectre:
> O speak to us of death, tell us its mysteries,
> Not here, not here, not in the hollow tomb,
> But at the Muse's fountain . . .
> By the plane trees you planted, in the sacred shade.

Even the most heroic of men must pass into death, but perhaps they live on in places that are somehow their own. More likely, Sacheverell fears, they will wake no more; for in his final lines he laments

> The heart is not a clock, it will not wind again,
> The dead are but dead, there is no use for them,
> They neither care, nor care not, they are only dead.

Sacheverell thought his *Canons of Giant Art* his best volume of poetry. Edith and Osbert were of like mind. Osbert expressed his admiration in person; Edith in a letter. "My darling," she wrote, "I'm more proud than I can possibly say. . . . You know what I've always known your poetry to be." She went on to recommend that Sacheverell should send Yeats a copy of *Canons*. Yeats, she effused, would lay hands on him as a result, but Sacheverell would simply have to put up with it. Unwittingly playing Cassandra, she added: "I feel writing to you rather as Yeats when he said to me, 'You don't mind what an ould, ould man like me says—but you mind what the biggest fool any editor has been able to find says.'"[12]

Modesty and decorum kept Sacheverell from sending Yeats a copy of *Canons*, as Edith had insisted he should. Eventually, she took it upon herself to do so for him. As she had anticipated, Yeats was properly impressed—so impressed, indeed, that he decided to include "Agamemnon's Tomb" in a collection of contemporary poetry he was compiling at the time. When the anthology was published in 1936 with the title *The Oxford Book of Modern Verse*, in an introduction Yeats even commented favorably upon Sacheverell's poetry. Prominent among those poets who preferred "to keep all the past their rival," he wrote, was "Sacheverell Sitwell with his *Canons of Giant Art*, written in the recently rediscovered 'sprung verse,' his main theme changes of colour, or historical phase, in Greece, Crete, India."[13]

Despite Yeats's high opinion of Sacheverell's *Canons*, most other poets and critics tended to ignore the work. The general indifference to his volume disturbed Sacheverell deeply. The times, he was sure, were against him. Those close to him wondered if he might try another book of poetry. He had bourne slings and arrows before, but now, he complained "there seemed simply no point in going on getting kicked in the pants."[14] Sacheverell wrote no poetry for publication for the next forty years.

The Whole Treatment

The poor reception Sacheverell's *Canons* had at the hands of critics was roughly equivalent to the reception accorded Osbert's third novel, *Miracle on Sinai*. There was one major difference, however. Instead of ignoring Osbert's novel when it was first published in 1934, as Sacheverell's *Canons* had been when published the year before, *Miracle on Sinai* was given the whole treatment, proving perhaps that poetry can easily be slighted though a work of fiction by an established novelist calls for evaluation.

"In spite of occasional crackles of wit," one critic declared, "*Miracle on Sinai* is the final denial of early promise. The truth is that all the puppets in the volume are . . . deader than smelts."[15] Others labeled the work "definitely lightweight,"[16] "a futile book,"[17] "nothing to give three cheers about."[18] Graham Greene found *Miracle on Sinai* especially disappointing. "Mr. Sitwell," he cautioned, "calls his novel a satire, but he has chosen as subjects figures who have only a literary existence. You cannot satirize puppets. . . ."[19] Keeping in mind that he had been on good terms with the Sitwells since his undergraduate days at Oxford in the early twenties, Greene, tempering his views a bit added, "Of course, there are some good jokes: but their brilliance cannot redeem a novel without a plan from a dull dilettanism."[20]

Osbert, pleased to learn that Greene gave approval to the "brilliance" of "some good jokes," was dismayed that he dismissed *Miracle on Sinai* as lacking "a plan." The frame on which the satire is built, Osbert thought, was one of the chief features of his novel. How clever, he still believed, to have brought together a cosmopolitan group of characters at a luxury hotel, the Aaron Palace, situated at the foot of Mount Sinai, and to have them all interact.

One day, for want of something to do, his characters climb to the summit of the mountain to enjoy a picnic. They are there but a short time when a mysterious storm cloud descends. After it lifts they discover two tablets of stone, upon which are graven ten new commandments. Sir Levy, Bart., M.P., a wealthy Jewish financier afflicted with megalomania, plays the part of a second Moses; but each picnic guest sees inscribed upon the tablets only what confirms his own dreams and desires. With delightful irony Osbert has them argue whether the injunctions are "Buy British," "Think Imperially," "Thou Shall Not be Repressed," "Safety First," or others of like description. Ultimately, the truth cannot be ascertained; for an ardent geologist, Professor Crotchester, beats the tablets to pieces in a vain attempt to obtain specimens of stone for research back at the Athenaeum.

Though all the characters are living beings, they are emblematic of matters Osbert felt a need to satirize—ruthless capitalism, Marxist socialism, fanatical militarism, extravagant scientism, societal morality, and institutionalized religion. Each representative and respected type who flourished in England between the two wars is cut deeply by Osbert's wit. In his seriocomic drama, Osbert concentrated on the faults and foibles of such characters as Lord Pridian, a press baron; Dr. Acquarius, a water diviner; Stuart Lollygo, a rabid communist; and Lady Helen Hornblower, a frequent ornament in the divorce courts. Each character, ridiculous and pathetic, is vivified in brittle absurdity.

A fanatical Muslim, Shereef Abdul, who is attended by his many wives, has a chance to put his beliefs into practice. From the tablets he had read: "There is No God but Allah; and Mohammed is the Prophet of God." What Shareef had seen on the tablets—in Arabic, of course—enjoins him to give the infidels twenty-four hours to accept his creed or suffer the consequences. If they refuse conversion, he will have to execute the men and care for their women in his harem. As Shareef's tribesmen surround Aaron Palace, only one member of the party escapes, a fradulent American medium, Madame Galactic. She flies off on a mail plane, leaving behind her tambourine, trumpet, and other spiritualistic accoutrements.

Osbert's satirical method, its strengths and weaknesses, is apparent in *Miracle on Sinai*. The novel is rich in Peacockian and Dickensian humor. Like another Thomas Love Peacock, Osbert had each of his type characters reveal himself through ludicrous thoughts and action. With the brush of a Dickens, Osbert delineated his characters in minute detail. Lord Pridian, for example, is "a placid, pot-bellied little mock-Buonaparte" who deludes himself into believing he is someone of great importance whereas he is really little more than "a money beetle";[21] Major-General Sir Rudyard, "who had quelled the budding mutiny at Melnaipore by giving the order to fire into 'the dirty, black-faced mob,' " now serves "as president of the new, and very popular, Society for the Prevention of Foreign Artists from Entering Britain or of Native Ones from Escaping from It";[22] and T. L. Enfelon is personified as an author with "a mild but petulant beard," who is always dressed in "loose shaggy clothes clinging to a giraffe-like body."[23]

Enfelon is an obvious caricature of D.H. Lawrence. Many of the other characters had been drawn from individuals Osbert had known, but they are not so clearly drawn as his portrait of Lawrence—nor of equal interest. A few of the characters are composites and of even less interest. Osbert thought otherwise, of course, for he devoted some thirty-six pages at the beginning of his novel to Dickensian portraits of his dramatis personae. Despite his elaborate portraiture, even the chief characters populating *Miracle on Sinai* are not fully realized, hardly the three-dimensional human beings one enjoys meeting in modern novels. His satirizations are so exaggerated, furthermore, that they border on the burlesque. If effective satire requires bulls-eye cleverness, it must be conceded that Osbert in *Miracle on Sinai* more often than not barely hit his targets.

In 1935, however, with the publication of his next book, *Penny Foolish*, Osbert proved that he was still capable of writing satire. This time in brief essays and sketches he concentrated on diverse subjects. His *Book of Tirades and Panegyrics*, as he subtitled the collection, is a criticism of events he found disquieting, an assault upon authors he disliked, and an animadversion of sundried matters. Seventy in number, the essays are in the main pungent and penetrating. One critic summed them up nicely when he commented that, despite Osbert's "self-sufficiency, his air of omniscience, and his occasional bad manners," *Penny Foolish* had not only "a style marked by grace" but "a crispness" that made reading his prose a delight.[24]

That critics would favor his essays and lambaste his *Miracle on Sinai* troubled Osbert. As much as he secretly desired universal acclaim, he convinced himself that what he wanted to express was of more importance than comments limited critics might offer about his work. Of the more than two dozen titles that he had already published, moreover, some had evinced a good response. Besides, he was only in his early forties. More than likely, he reflected, he had not yet really hit his stride, that he had several good years left to write the many books still within him.

Chapter Eight

Books of Great Beauty

A Violent Success

In the spring of 1934, about the same time that Osbert was bearing up under the negative reviews accorded his *Miracle on Sinai*, Edith was attempting to complete a study of Queen Victoria. Aware of the caustic criticism Osbert's novel provoked, and sensitive to the lack of response Sacheverell's *Canons of Giant Art* had had the year before, Edith was especially concerned about her fourth volume of prose. In a letter to Osbert she even questioned why she allowed her publisher to persuade her to do a biography of "that old bore . . . that bloody Victoria."[1]

Neither *Alexander Pope*, *Bath*, nor *English Eccentrics* had had as wide a sale as Edith had hoped, but each had sold; and Faber and Faber anticipated a wider market for a sensitive study of Britain's "Empress of the World." While not sharing her publisher's high hopes, Edith convinced herself that her biography would be no worse than Lytton Strachey's *Queen Victoria*, published some fourteen years before. Though Strachey had been a respected Bloomsbury figure, as Edith viewed him he seemed "to have been cut out of very thin cardboard" (*TC*, 95), the same kind of cardboard he had used to fabricate his life of Victoria. Strachey, in turn, had little love for Edith. In his own vituperative fashion, he had once described her nose as "longer than an ant-eaters" and her poetry as "absurd stuff."[2]

Far from being the fiasco she feared, when *Victoria of England* was published early in 1936, her biography—which she had deprecated as "larger than the London telephone directory and just about as dull"—became, as she declared in a letter to Osbert, "a violent success."[3] Nothing she had written before enjoyed such instant and wide acclaim. Since the work had originally been undertaken more for money than for art, she was delighted that it did so well. The hopes of her publisher were fully realized. Printing after printing sold out. Edith is "in transports," Sacheverell remarked, after learning that her "first best-seller" had brought a substantial royalty check from Faber and Faber. "Isn't it lovely for her?"[4]

John Sparrow declared *Victoria of England* "a book of great beauty."[5] Most critics thought it a sincere and moving character study of a great woman. A few dismissed it as neither biography, nor history, nor as objective in approach as it should have been. Its readers, however, agreed that the work was clever and entertaining. If her dramatized portrait was not a full history of Victoria's reign, it was not meant to be. If she had failed to deal in depth with political questions, as she herself had pointed out in her preface, academics more competent than she had already done so. Whatever *Victoria of England* may lack in scholarship is more than compensated for by Edith's imaginative and innovative reconstruction of known facts.

Edith's success with *Victoria of England*, it has been theorized, was basically a consequence of her not having any special feelings for her subject: "There was no reason for any identification with Victoria, as there had been with Pope, and the book was better written as a result."[6] A childhood impression of the queen, nonetheless, always lingered in her imagination. The incident was significant enough for Edith to recall it in her autobiography.

One day Edith, who was only four years of age at the time, was walking with her nurse through a garden, "under . . . pale green light, that was like water flowing, of an eucalyptus tree," when her nurse suddenly turned and intoned: "*Her* carriage is coming. You must curtesy." The barouche contained an old woman in widow's weeds. Edith respectfully curtsied and received in return an impressive bow. Only then did her nurse explain that the old woman was the queen. Many years later, Edith summed up her encounter with Victoria with the observation: "I was curtesying to an age, a world, that was passing" (*TC*, 23–24).

In her biography, however, Edith was not so much concerned with the age that had passed as she was with the queen herself, her childhood, her relations with her family, her ministers, her servants, her subjects. In only one rather macabre chapter entitled "March Past" did Edith focus on the Victorian poor, those doomed from their very birth to a life of pauperism and deprivation. The graphic descriptions of the homeless, the beggars, the slum dwellers, the indigent, and the exploited she drew from Engls's *Conditions of the Working Class in England*, which he had prepared for the Ashley Committee in 1844. With the same compassion she first manifested in *Gold Coast Customs* seven years before, Edith wrote of the pathetic victims of the industrial revolution: the factory workers, the weavers, the grinders, the potters, the miners, the abject children.

For major parts of her study, Edith relied heavily upon such works as Henry Hector Bolitho's *Albert the Good* (1932), A. Ponsonby's *Queen Victoria* (1933), Roger Fulford's *The Royal Dukes: The Father and Uncles of Queen Victoria* (1933), and Edward F. Benson's *Queen Victoria* (1935). How much she drew from Strachey's nonhagiographic study *Queen Victoria* (1921) became matter for debate. Those who complained she had plagiarized Strachey maintained that in the process she molded the queen and everyone else into wax fruit. Anticipating such captious criticism, in her preface Edith acknowledged that she had utilized a common stock of information about Victoria but that she had done her best to render necessarily similar material a different treatment.

More objective critics, while acknowledging Strachey's undeniable influence upon Edith's work, found her version of Victoria warmer and broader. They pointed out that, unlike Strachey, who tended to mock and demean here and there in his biography, especially in his depiction of Albert, Edith was not that concerned with the prince consort's necessarily inferior status. Strachey, furthermore, dealt rather summarily with Victoria after the death of Albert while Edith preferred to amplify the character of the widow of Windsor during the second half of her reign and to dwell particularly upon her relations with her children and grandchildren.

The average reader cared little about charges of plagiarism that so delighted the academics. Debates over the matter left the issue unresolved; for every charge those anxious to vilify Edith's study presented, her apologists provided a suitable response. One pundit found a middle ground. As far as he was concerned, *Victoria of England* was an excellent consolidation of all that was known about the Queen: a volume with "a Stracheyan touch . . . and Sitwell trimmings."[7]

The trimmings, the sprightly descriptions, the splendid enthusiasms, the psychological probings account in large measure for the enormous success of Edith's biography. Even more important is the skill evident in her rendering of the life of such a strong personality as Victoria in readily understandable components. The reader willingly suspends all disbeliefs as Edith wholly convinces him that she was somehow able to comprehend all that engaged Victoria's attention. From Victoria's first night as queen, as an eighteen-year-old girl dreaming of greatness, to the final meditations of the aged monarch sinking into her final sleep, Edith enables the reader to fathom the mind of a remarkable woman. Edith's ability to convince the reader that she was privy to all that was most important to Victoria's active mind encouraged a critic for the *Saturday Review of Literature* to recommend that, whatever encomiums any other biography of the queen, including that of Strachey, may deserve, Edith had still "painted the most living, and hence appealing, portrait of Queen Victoria yet written."[8]

Out of the Doldrums

The twenties had been Edith's decade, but during the early years of the thirties she, Osbert, and Sacheverell suffered a partial eclipse. They went on working as diligently as ever, giving virtually all their time and energy to their art, but the excitement their books had once generated had all but disappeared. Was it simply that they had grown older? Times change and it was now 1936. They were no longer *enfants terrible*. Edith was forty-nine, Osbert forty-four, and Sacheverell thirty-nine. Had their careers peaked too early? There was a period when all three Sitwells feared their reputations might diminish even further.

Fortunately for Edith, the adulation accorded her *Victoria of England* was exactly what she needed to lift her out of the doldrums. With her enthusiasms rekindled she managed to overcome many of the self-doubts about herself and her art that had plagued her for several years. She even contemplated writing a novel, one through which she could further extirpate any remaining anxieties and lingering personal griefs. Though she had suffered many disappointments and had been buffeted about by critics, one success now began to follow another. A request from Yeats to include some of her poetry in his forthcoming edition of *The Oxford Book of Modern Verse* brought with it a special measure of satisfaction.

Yeats, who had always been keen on Edith's work, often informed her of his admiration in various letters they exchanged. In a radio broadcast he made in 1936, he publicly stated his views. First, he defended Edith against some of the severe charges that such critics as Wyndham Lewis, Geoffrey Grigson, G.W. Stonier, and F.R.

Leavis had leveled against her. Then he went on to praise her in his own genial way. Finally, he concluded: "Miss Sitwell . . . seems to be an important poet."[9] There was no doubt in his mind that she fully merited the medal of the Royal Society of Literature that he had advocated for her two years before.

As for what poems of Edith's to include in his anthology, Yeats could not readily decide. In a letter to the poet Dorothy Wellesley he revealed that he was rereading all of Edith's poetry and that he was finding it difficult to select representative works. One poem is so dependent upon another, he confided, "it would [be] like cutting a piece out of a tapestry."[10] Ultimately, he chose "The Hambone and the Heart," "Colonel Fantock," "Ass-Face," "The Lament for Edward Blastock," and long selections from "The Sleeping Beauty" and "Gold Coast Customs."

Edith was as pleased with Yeats's selections of her poems as he had been with what she had written about him in her *Aspects of Modern Poetry* (1934). He was familiar with her *Poetry and Criticism* (1925) and had read with considerable interest her Pleasures of Poetry series: *Milton and the Augustan Age* (1930), *The Romantic Revival* (1931), and *The Victorian Period* (1932). Chronologically, criticism of the literature of the modern period had to follow, and Yeats had been curious about what Edith might write about their contemporaries—and especially what she might have to say about him.

A brief perusal of Edith's *Aspects of Modern Poetry* indicated to Yeats that every time she mentioned his name it was done with reverence. A closer examination of the book revealed that it had four distinct parts. In the opening section, "Pastors and Masters," Edith assailed any and all who had questioned her art. In particular, she singled out the three critics who had most disparaged her as a poet and as a person—Lewis, Grigson, and Leavis. They had cut her so often and so deeply she could neither forgive nor forget their trespasses against her.

Six individual chapters make up the second section. Here she focused in turn upon the half dozen poets she held were most worthy of attention: Gerard Manley Hopkins, W. B. Yeats, W. H. Davies, T. S. Eliot, Ezra Pound and Sacheverell Sitwell. The most perceptive chapters treat Yeats, Eliot, and Pound. Edith's discussion of Hopkins's extraordinary visual sense is quite provocative. Her least successful chapters are those on Davies and her brother. Edith was too

cloyingly sympathetic toward Davies and far too technical and tedious in her treatment of Sacheverell's verse.

The third section of *Aspects of Modern Poetry*, "Innovations in
Prose," strictly speaking, does not belong in a critical discussion of
modern verse, but Edith felt she had to include her response to the
experimental work of James Joyce and Edith Stein. Nor did she
think it proper to ignore entirely "the younger poets." In an "Envoi"
that brings the volume to a close, she concentrated upon such figures
as e. e. cummings, C. Day Lewis, Ronald Bottrall, and W. H.
Auden. The only reason she did not react more favorably to these
"New Verse" poets lies in the conjecture that she was not quite
prepared to admit them into the literary pantheon.

At the time she was even unprepared to say anything compli-
mentary about the efforts of Dylan Thomas. In *Aspects of Modern
Poetry*, in fact, she attacked his poem "Our Eunuch Dreams" and
failed to name him as its author. In a letter to John Sparrow, she
had already dismissed Thomas as "a youth who ought to be dashed
off to a psycho-analyst before worse befalls. . . ."[11] Later, however,
Edith did an about-face. She began to praise Thomas extravagantly
and convinced herself that she had discovered him. When they first
met, Thomas was so in awe of Edith that all went well. Eventually,
he misbehaved in her presence and a falling-out ensued.

Edith always enjoyed playing the role of sybilline adviser, but
once Thomas's reputation began to mushroom, he made it difficult
for her to do so. After word got back to Edith that he was doing
ruthless imitations of her in London pubs, she declared that their
relationship was over. At first, she sought revenge. Later, when she
learned of his early death from alcoholism she was filled with re-
morse. Finally, in her autobiography she wrote more about Thomas
than about any other poet who had merited her attention (*TC*, 179,
198–208, 212). One of her most worthy accomplishments, Edith
assured herself, was her early patronage of Dylan Thomas, her discovery of, assistance to, and influence on his erratic genius.

Creativity and Productivity

Mainly because of the success of her *Victoria of England*, 1936 was
a good year for Edith. It was also a year of significant achievement
for Sacheverell—not that his efforts brought him monetary rewards.
Though he published three volumes, their total sales were miniscule

in contrast to those of Edith's biography of Victoria. Sacheverell's three volumes gave further evidence, if any were needed, of both his creativity and productivity.

The most important of Sacheverell's books published in 1936 was his *Collected Poems*, a volume of nearly 600 pages in fairly small print, prefaced by a long essay by Edith. In her *Aspects of Modern Poetry* she had devoted a full chapter to her brother's verse, but she had even more to say about his technical achievements. The structure of Sacheverell's poems, it seemed to Edith, was the important thing. More concerned for some reason with his "texture" than his themes, she observed in her introduction: "Changes in rhythm, some great, some subtle, are effected in Mr. Sitwell's verse by the varying depth, breadth, height or shallowness of the pauses, and these are . . . largely the result of texture."[12]

Over some thirty-five pages, Edith continued to expatiate upon Sacheverell's skillful use of caesuras, his shifting vowel schemes, the musicality of his verse, the majesty of his diction. "We are in need of a test whether a man cares for poetry as poetry," she stressed, "or whether he cares for it as expressing some sentiment, or conveying some meaning, which is agreeable or seems respectful to him."[13] Edith's labored prosodic anaylsis of Sacheverell's verse was her way of demonstrating that he truly cared for poetry *qua* poetry, that, moreover, "the sensuous beauty of Mr. Sitwell's poetry is unsurpassed."[14]

In her long introduction, Edith had much to say about Sacheverell's poetic craftsmanship but little about his shortcomings. Far too often, for example, he was too expansive—if not discursive. Though Sacheverell could easily be as esoterically allusive as Eliot, Pound, or Yeats, he could not manipulate metaphor as deftly as they did in their best poems. After reading Sacheverell's *Collected Poems*, even one of his most ardent devotees, John Smith, commented that the volume "suffers from the gravest problem of the romantic poet, who in the lyric can be so easily seduced away from simple eloquence by a prettiness of language."[15]

When his *Collected Poems* failed to receive the approval that Edith, Osbert, Yeats, and a handful of critics thought the volume deserved, Sacheverell was so disappointed that he feared his career as a poet was over. Fortunately, he had many other irons in the fire—two of which he forged in 1936, *Dance of the Quick and the Dead* and *Conversation Pieces.*

In the *Dance of the Quick and the Dead*, Sacheverell indulged in speculations on the majesty of art at loggerheads with the humdrum restrictions placed upon life. This *Entertainment of the Imagination*, as he subtitled the volume, allows glimpses of human misery on the one hand and of imaginary paradises of spirit and sense on the other. Implicit in all that is dealt with in this intellectual fantasia is the reminder that art is humanity's strongest bulwark against the tide of time. In his "entertainment of the imagination" Sacheverell demonstrated that the artist, the poet, by some power of the imagination enables others to discriminate "the quick from the dead."

In *Southern Baroque Art, The Gothick North*, and *Spanish Baroque Art*, Sacheverell revealed his abiding love affair with continental art. *Conversation Pieces*, as its subtitle makes clear, is *A Survey of English Domestic Portraits and Their Painters*; accordingly, he wrote of Hogarth, Gainsborough, Stubbs, Patch, Constable, and Turner, as well as of a host of minor figures who portrayed the English country gentleman surrounded by his children, dogs and horses, pictures and musical instruments, pilasters, and fields. In his discourse upon the magnificence of such eighteenth- and early nineteenth-century paintings, Sacheverell made no attempt to be conclusive, though the original quality of much of what he had to say in *Conversation Pieces* helped solidify his reputation as one of England's foremost art historians.

Narrative Pictures further revealed Sacheverell's interest in the English scene. In this study he concerned himself essentially with the pictures of incident and anecdote painted during the previous two hundred years, examining at length the moral and didactic implications of certain paintings that held significant meaning for him. Along the way, he showed his admiration for Victorian art—of which the study was then in its infancy—writing with gusto about certain Pre-Raphaelite paintings in a manner reminiscent of Ruskin at his best. In brief, *Narrative Pictures*, like its companion *Conversation Pieces*, is a further vision of art and life that Sacheverell managed to communicate so successfully to his readers.

Careers to Worry About

Edith and Osbert, pleased as they were with Sacheverell's creativity and productivity, were concerned that his recent books hardly repaid the effort that went into them. Keenly aware that their

younger brother, having a wife and two sons to support, was continually short of funds, Edith and Osbert consoled themselves that
sooner or later he would produce a best-seller. They were proud of
Sacheverell's reputation as the family's intellectual, but that did not
lessen their uneasiness about his financial future. Apart from a small
legacy, Sacheverell had to rely upon the sale of his books to sustain
himself and his family. That he managed to set up a home, to
entertain a circle of friends, and even to travel wherever his interest
led him is a tribute to his resourcefulness. In certain ways he proved
more resourceful than either Edith or Osbert, who now had their
own careers to worry about.

In 1937, Edith and Osbert were both working on novels, neither
of which, as it turned out, did much for their respective careers.
Edith's first work of fiction, which she entitled *I Live under a Black
Sun*, came out in September. Osbert's fourth novel, which he called
Those Were the Days, was not published until the spring of the
following year. The triumphs that both had devoutly wished for
never came. The reviews were polite, but neither novel found a
wide audience.

In a foreword to *I Live under a Black Sun*, Edith explained that
its narrative was based upon Jonathan Swift's relationship with the
two women central to his life, Stella and Vanessa, with the time
framework and certain major details altered. One major transfor-
mation is that of period, for the story is set in the twentieth century
with World War I serving as backdrop. The time warp was undoubtedly influenced by Virginia Woolf's traversing linear duration
in *Orlando*, *The Years*, and other novels, but Edith, in transposing
all her material to the contemporary, did not use to advantage
flashback and timeslip techniques favored by Woolf.

Into a complex tapestry, Edith wove many of her own private
experiences. Most of the characters in her roman à clef, consequently,
can be identified, although some of them have dual identities.
Behind the figure of Jonathan Hare, for example, lurk both Swift
and Pavel Tchelitchew. Merged into the character of the brilliant
but eccentric eighteenth-century cleric is the equally eccentric and
brilliant twentieth-century Russian artist.

Gertrude Stein had introduced Edith to Tchelitchew in 1927
while she was in Paris to take in Sacheverell's ballet, *The Triumph
of Neptune*. The artist found Edith fascinating; on her part, it was
love at first sight. Little did either suspect that their relationship

over the next thirty years would distress them both deeply. Edith, who came to look upon herself as Tchelitchew's muse, was flattered to sit for six portraits and a sculpture of her head in wax and wire. Had she not posed for the artist, it is unlikely that she would have written *I Live under a Dark Sun*; nor would their relationship have developed to the point it did.

At first, they enjoyed each other's company and were frequently together. On Edith's side, she had good reason to be jealous of Tchelitchew's attachment to Allen Tanner, an American pianist, and a string of other male friends. Then, too, she came to realize that Tchelitchew was an opportunist who accepted her friendship and patronage but gave little in return. Marriage, it slowly dawned upon her, was out of the question. Not only was she forty years old, but she had to face the many problems that sprang from the artist's homosexuality. On Tchelitchew's side, despite an initial attraction for Edith, the simple truth is that he probably never really cared for her.[16]

Once the character of Jonathan Hare is identified with Tchelitchew, it becomes clear that in writing about him Edith gave vent to the anguish of their strained relationship. The part that the artist demanded Edith play, for example, is understood from Jonathan's words early in the novel: "Every human being needs to be believed in—I have never doubted my greatness. . . . I must have someone who believes in me, who is ready to give up her will to me. . . ."[17] Edith was prepared to submit entirely to Tchelitchew, and it broke her heart that he never asked her to do so. Giving voice to such concerns, Edith has one character in the novel affirm that she devoted her whole life, "the whole of her existence, all [her] thoughts to Jonathan for years . . . oh yes, for long years"; and as she speaks such words, "the knowledge of the truth . . . , the realization of the nobility of that selfless sacrifice grows upon her."[18]

In the novel, the heroine Anna Marton, who sacrifices all for love, is on one level Swift's beloved Stella (Esther Johnson) and on another Edith herself. Anna's sacrifice is betrayed when Jonathan takes up with Esther Vanelden, Swift's Vanessa (Hester Vanhomrigh), who represents the other side of Edith, violently and irretrievably in love with Jonathan. When Esther pleads for his love, he spurns her. After her misery becomes habitual, Jonathan complains: "You have allowed it to grow on you . . . until it has become a necessity to you. It is . . . something you indulge in as the poor indulge in sorrow because it is their only luxury."[19] Those familiar with the life of Swift can appreciate how closely Edith's relationship with Tchelitchew parallels the story of the Dean and the two women in his life.

As for the other characters in the novel, it is obvious that the erratic politician Sir Henry Rotherham, an agnostic who says his prayers every night, was modeled after Edith's own father, Sir George. Wyndham Lewis can be seen in the sinister politician Henry DeBingham. Lesser characters are composites drawn from life and Edith's fertile imagination. Those in the subplot, such as Susan Daw, seem pure fiction. It is Susan, incidentally, daughter of a mean and bullying father, who runs away from home after her fiancé is killed in the war. Once again, Edith played upon a love-hate relationship, for Susan marries the German soldier who had killed the man she had originally hoped to marry. Finally, this minor plot is linked to the main narrative when Susan finds employment in Anna's household in Ireland.

A Cool Reception

The cool reception that *I Live under a Black Sun* received was a major disappointment to Edith. Having put so much of herself into the novel, she felt that it had to be far more successful than her *Victoria of England*, which she undertook more to satisfy her publisher than her own literary aspirations. Virtually all of the 4,000 copies of *I Live under a Black Sun* that made up a first printing sold, but there was little likelihood of a second printing. Upset by the indifference of most critics, Edith was especially annoyed by a review in the influential *Times Literary Supplement*. "It seems that all the Pipsqueakery are after me in full squeak . . . ," she mourned.[20]

The unidentified critic writing for the *Times Literary Supplement* rejected Edith's novel as "uneven," its prose "overburdened." The alteration of the time frame, he confessed, confused him to such an extent that he did not know if he were reading " a fairy tale" or "the substance of a nightmare."[21] Had the critic known that Edith had incorporated her relationship with Tchelitchew within the labyrinthine passages of the novel, would it have made a difference? He still could have rightfully focused on Edith's confusion of intent and execution, her meandering plot and stilted dialogue.

Edith took comfort from Evelyn Waugh's reaction. He described

I Live under a Black Sun as "a magnesium flame in a cavern, immediately and abundantly beautiful." The novel was such that "it defied cursory treatment" and had "to be read patiently . . . more than once." Unaware that Swift was a stand-in for Tchelitchew, Waugh proclaimed that Edith had seen "deep into a tortured soul, to horror beneath horror," and he summed up *I Live under a Black Sun* as "a terrifying book."[22] William Empson, on the other hand, was of the opinion that Edith had made Swift's pathological misery seem "normal and typical."[23] These antithetical views of Waugh and Empson demonstrate that even the most careful readers did not know how to respond to *I Live under a Black Sun*.

Never one to take criticism lightly, every time her novel was attacked, Edith was prepared to defend it. Why had she put Swift in contemporary clothes? "Because the spirit of the modern world is power gone mad," she responded. "And Swift was power gone mad."[24] Was *I Live under a Black Sun* more of a biography than a work of fiction? "I beg you to believe that I don't consider it a novel," she gave for an answer. "It is an allegory."[25] But when pressed, she refused to disclose the allegory. Possibly she best summed up her own feelings about the work when she labeled it her "ewe lamb," and then added: "I feel about it as I do about my poetry— I mean a personal feeling, as if it was part of myself. . . ."[26] *I Live under a Black Sun* embodies that part of Edith which ultimately forced her to accept the hopelessness of her love for Pavel Tchelitchew. Writing the novel also made her face the sad fact that her forte was not fiction.

More Novelist Than Poet

Despite the poor reception of Osbert's *Those Were the Days*, a fictional evocation of vanished life in London and prewar Florence, he still believed that he was more of a novelist than poet. Shortly before publication of this fourth work of fiction, which he had hopes would be his most successful work, he provided an editor at Macmillan with a long list of friends who were to be sent author's copies. Osbert's list included the names of Somerset Maughan, John Sparrow, Maurice Baring, and the queen.[27] It is interesting to speculate on their initial reactions to *Those Were the Days*. Beyond speculation is the fact that the novel sold poorly. Again Osbert wrote his publisher, this time Harold Macmillian himself. "I am only sorry that

my . . . novel . . . should not have been a whopping success,"
he lamented. "I am so tired of 'moral success. . . .' I believe it to
be my best book: author's vanity, I suppose."[28]

Osbert had done his best to write a significant piece of work, a
novel that would rival, if not surpass, his *Before the Bombardment*.
Though he labored long and hard over *Those Were the Days*, it
remained deficient in plot, characterization—and interest. His words
were beautifully polished, but to concentrate on the effectiveness of
his language would be like picking the raisins out of a pasty pudding.
The story of young Joanna Freemartin's being recalled to Newborough from her finishing school in Florence because of the Great
War was, at best, a flimsy peg on which to hang a 540-page
narrative.

Joanna's interactions with a host of characters are of little consequence. Her interest in Stanley Esar, who vigorously repulses her,
provides a bit of humor, as does Osbert's filling the plot with all
sorts of trivialities, most of which he apparently experienced himself.
One of Joanna's relatives, for example, after finding a shell splinter
embedded in her wall, decides to present it to a young officer about
to embark for France. In like fashion, when Lady Ida, Osbert's
mother, traveled from Scarborough to London to wish her son well
before he left for the Western Front, she presented him with a shell
splinter, souvenir of the bombardment of Scarborough, for a good
luck token (*L*, 76).

Trivial in itself, this shell splinter incident is indicative of Osbert's
reminiscing about experiences that he would later utilize in memoirs
he was planning to fashion into a book. Before he seriously got
around to what was to become a five-volume autobiography, however, there were several other projects he had to complete. One at
immediate hand was his part in the Northcliffe Lectures that he,
Edith, and Sacheverell had been invited to deliver at the University
of London.

The adverse opinions of certain critics notwithstanding, toward
the end of the thirties the Sitwells were widely regarded as paladins
of English literature. As such, they were requested to deliver a series
of joint lectures on "Aspects of National Genius." To speak before
the faculty and students of London University was of course an
honor, and they determined to make the most of their opportunity.
After a brief discussion among themselves, Edith agreed to speak
on poetry, Osbert on prose, and Sacheverell on art and architecture.

Osbert spoke first. Though he had written a monograph on Dickens some six years before, he still had a great deal more to say about his favorite author. In his *Dickens* (1932), Osbert had focused in particular on the Victorian novelist's gifts of observation and his ability to portray character. In his first lecture, "Dickens and the Modern Novel," Osbert dealt with the influence that the author of so many wonderful novels had exerted upon contemporary fiction. An obvious inference from what Osbert had to say on the subject was that he was in a direct line of descent from Dickens, whose power of vivifying a character even he could not match. In his second lecture, Osbert followed up with the subject "The Modern Novel: Its Causes and Cure."

Edith's contribution to the Northcliffe Lectures were two talks on "Three Eras of Modern Poetry," in which she attempted an analysis of the "musicality" of contemporary verse. What she had to say was a further extension of some early ideas of prosody that she had first voiced in her monograph *Poetry and Criticism* a dozen years before and then embellished in her *Aspects of Poetry* in 1934.

Sacheverell, the last to speak, offered two rather businesslike, information-filled discourses. The first, "George Cruikshank," covered the work of the famous nineteenth-century English caricaturist and illustrator. The second, "Paladin England," summarized the influence of the great sixteenth-century Italian artist Andrea Palladio upon British architecture.

On the whole, the lectures went well and were well received. When they were published under the title *Trio* in 1938, it appeared that the Sitwells were as unified as they had been fifteen years before at the first public performance of *Facade*. Regrettably, they were not. As in so many other families in which siblings drift apart, so had Edith, Osbert, and Sacheverell. They were never jealous of one another's success—and they united whenever one of their works was attacked by critics—but each had a private life to lead.

Edith, at low ebb, had her uneasy love for Pavel Tchelitchew to deal with. Osbert, suffering from debilitating attacks of gout, was at odds with David Horner, a good-looking young man with whom Osbert had formed a close relationship. And Sacheverell, though happily married, was finding it difficult to live the style of life he believed his station entitled him to. On top of everything, 1938 was the year that Hitler marched into Austria and all Europe was a tinderbox.

Chapter Nine
War and Victory
More Than Escapism

In 1939, though he feared war was imminent, Osbert went on with his work and completed a book that he had been laboring over for several years—*Escape with Me! An Oriental Sketch Book*. Essentially a journal of his travels in the Far East, embellished with personal anecdotes and literary and social comments, the volume records many of his impressions of the beauty and wonder of Cambodia and Peking.

Late in 1934, accompanied by David Horner, Osbert set out for the Orient. For years he had longed to travel through the Far East, to soak in its culture, and, as he was later to note in an introduction to *Escape with Me!*, he wanted to experience the wonders of the Orient before it perished. He was not disappointed.

Osbert found Angkor fascinating, one of "the chief wonders of the world today, one of the summits to which human genius had aspired in stone."[1] Peking was even more to his liking and turned him into an ardent Sinophile. In this traditional capital of China, he called upon his old friend Harold Acton, who had taken up residence there. Mainly because of Acton, a dandy turned Sinologist, Osbert lingered in China for several months studying Oriental art and architecture.

Most of *Escape with Me!* was written on the spot, but Osbert had so many wonderful experiences in Angkor and Peking that some of them were written from emotions recollected in tranquility. Despite the imperative title, the book was more than a long essay on escapism. So impressed were critics with Osbert's *Oriental Sketch Book* that virtually all who reviewed it wrote of it in glowing terms. Hugh Walpole spoke for many when he labeled *Escape with Me!* one of the best travel books written in English over the previous fifty years.[2]

Osbert could take comfort from the wonderful reviews his *Escape with Me!* received, but when Hitler invaded Poland on 1 September

1939 he feared that the tragedies he had witnessed in Flanders some twenty-two years before would soon overwhelm the entire world. He was now forty-six, in uncertain health, and actually less than enthusiastic for the leadership that his old enemy Winston Churchill hoped to provide now that England and France had declared war on Germany. Churchill, as far as Osbert was concerned, was still the same bloodstained demagogue he had satirized twenty years before in *The Winstonburg Line*.

With few options open to him, Osbert decided to retreat to the Sitwell estate at Renishaw and wait out the war. Edith soon joined him there. Sacheverell preferred to remain with his wife at Weston Hall, one of the Sitwell manor houses in Northamptonshire. Sacheverell joined the Home Guards, but Edith and Osbert chose to cloister themselves at Renishaw. Like all Britons, they were horrified by the fall of France and the subsequent blitz on London. To bolster their spirits, they often complained that the war was such a dreadful waste of time, talent, and life; yet, respectful of one another's individual relationships, they seldom spoke of David Horner, who, being of military age, entered the Air Ministry, or of Pavel Tchelitchew, who fled to the states.

To pass their days, Edith concentrated her attention on three anthologies; Osbert on a volume of short stories. Edith's first volume, rather brazenly entitled *Edith Sitwell's Anthology*, was published early in 1940; her second, *Poems Old and New*, toward the end of that year; and her third, *Look! the Sun*, the following year. Each sold moderately well and would have been conveniently put aside had not *Edith Sitwell's Anthology* begun a little war of its own.

One reviewer for a left-wing journal, *Reynolds News*, reacted antagonistically. Other than complaining that the volume was too heavy to hold, and suggesting that Edith's 160-page critical introduction could well be omitted from future editions, he judged her anthology a delightful bedside book. But then he could not resist being clever and hypercritical. "Among the literary curiosities of the 1920's," he averred, "will be the vogue of the Sitwells, the sister and two brothers whose energy and self-assurance pushed them into a position which their merits could not have done."[3]

Not content with one salvo, he fired another: "One brother wrote amusing political verse. The sister produced a life of Alexander Pope. Now oblivion has claimed them and they are remembered with a kindly if slightly cynical smile."[4] To be denigrated literary

curiosities of the 1920s was offensive enough, but the Sitwells could
hardly tolerate their being assigned to "oblivion." Having a *prima
facie* case for libel, they decided to sue. *Reynolds News* preferred to
settle out of court, but the Sitwells determined to go to trial. Besides
any publicity they might derive from the case, they reasoned that
Reynolds News had to be taught a good lesson. It was. Edith, Osbert,
and Sacheverell won the day.[5]

To what extent the legal victory the Sitwells had may have influenced critics to treat Osbert's next book so kindly is open to
question; but when his *Open the Door*, a volume of seventeen short
stories, was published in the fall of 1940, it received highly favorable
reviews, far better reviews than his *Dumb-Animals*, another volume
of stories, had received when published eleven years before. The
critics, however, were less enthusiastic about a novel, *A Place of
One's Own*, published in the same year as *Open the Door*.

In truth, *A Place of One's Own*, a gothic tale of a haunted house
in Newborough, wherein a daft old woman had apparently committed suicide, has little about it to excite serious readers of quality
fiction. Even Osbert regarded the novel as little more than clever
entertainment. Gainsborough Studios, convinced that as entertainment the novel had the requisite ingredients for a good film, purchased the work. When finally produced in 1945, *A Place of One's
Own* enjoyed a successful run—its success assured by Bernard Knowles
directing such stars as Margaret Lockwood, James Mason, Dennis
Price, and Dulcie Gray in the leading roles.

Something to Write About

During the period that Edith assembled her anthologies and Osbert worked on his fiction, Sacheverell busily labored over the kind
of books he preferred to write—three of which were published in
1940. The first was *Mauretania*, a volume that grew out of notes
and memories of his trip to North Africa eleven years before. The
second was *Poltergeists*, a subject of interest from the days he first
learned that his father had attended meetings of the National Association of Spiritualists. The third was *Sacred and Profane Love*, a
journey into the realm of art and the lives of artists.

In *Sacred and Profane Love* Sacheverell paid tribute to the consummate artist he knew best, his own sister. Edith he remembered as
"a tall thin young woman in a pelisse of green sheepskin and a wide-

brimmed hat, who walks between the hedges upon the smoother grass. She has sloping shoulders, and picks her way among fallen twigs."[6] Added to this visual image of Edith that he always treasured in his memory was the thought that "from her shadow the woods leads on into poetry. For her love is poetry, she lives within a phrase."[7]

Edith was of course delighted with such a tribute; indeed, Sacheverell's words about her in his *Sacred and Profane Love* may have had something to do with her trying another volume of verse, her first in more than ten years. From the time she completed *Gold Coast Customs* in 1929 to 1940, she composed little serious verse. Now, encouraged by Sacheverell's words about her love for poetry and roused to compassion by the war, she felt she had something significant to write about: the terrible suffering brought about by the air raids on London. Her self-imposed period of silence as a poet was over; so, too, as a poet, her "time of experiments was done."[8]

When she began to turn her full attention to poetry once again, she concerned herself essentially with "the state of the world, of the terrible rain . . . falling alike upon guilty and guiltless, upon Dives and Lazarus."[9] She determined to write of "the sufferings of Christ, the Starved Man hung upon the Cross, the God of the Poor Man, who bears in His Heart all wounds."[10] As a consequence, in one of her earliest war poems, "Still Falls the Rain," published in the 6 September 1941 issue of the *Times Literary Supplement*, she incorporated her thoughts on the bombs raining from the sky with the sufferings of Christ.

Prayerlike, her poem begins

> Still falls the Rain—
> Dark as the world of man, black as our loss—
> Blind as the nineteen hundred and forty nails
> Upon the Cross.

The rain is like the blood that flowed from the wounded side of "the Starved Man hung upon the Cross." And

> Still falls the Rain—
> Then—O Ile leape up to my God: who pulls me doune—
> See, see where Christ's blood streams in the firmament:
> It flows from the Brow we nailed upon the tree.

With the coming of dawn the sacred blood may bring redemption; for "Then sounds the voice of One who like the heart of man / Was once a child who among beasts has lain." Christ still stands ready to forgive: "Still do I love, still shed my innocent light, my Blood for them."

Edith was the first British poet to write movingly of the horrors of World War II. "Still Falls the Rain" antedated Dylan Thomas's "Refusal to Mourn," Louis MacNeice's "Brother Fire," and C. D. Lewis's "Word Over All." Not only was "Still Falls the Rain" first in time, but several critics held it first in quality. C. M. Bowra pronounced it "the most profound and moving poem . . . written in English about the war."[11] Bowra was not alone in his judgment. Benjamin Britten was so moved by "Still Falls the Rain" that he set it to music he called "Canticle III."

In 1942, when "Still Falls the Rain" was published with some twenty other poems that also took their origin from the war and Edith's anagogical approach to suffering, it continued to create quite a stir. *Street Songs*, as she entitled her new volume, caught the spotlight. No longer could Edith be dismissed as the frivolous figure who had written *Facade*; now she was widely hailed as a deep and serious poet. "Her work has been a contribution to the intellectual life of the time," wrote Mary Colum. "She has not been like so many contemporary versifiers, 'the idle singer of an empty day.' "[12]

John Lehmann went a step further. During a broadcast over the BBC he claimed that Edith's was "an inspired voice that spoke for all the spiritual distress and longing of an agonized generation, with . . . a breath of vision and an artistic maturity . . ."[13] Elizabeth Drew also commented upon Edith's "deepening . . . poetic vision." What impressed Drew in particular was the *Street Songs* had "a purity of tone, and variety of effect" that could be "powerful or tender, mysterious or simple," and always "uniformly perfect in its formal beauty."[14]

Macmillan regretted that it had restricted *Street Songs* to an initial printing of only 1,500 copies. Over the next few months three additional printings also sold out. How could Edith fail to be delighted with her newfound popularity! Suddenly, during the madness of a war, readers found sanity in her poetry. The universality of her themes in *Street Songs*—the futility of battle, the materialism of mankind, the abiding love of Christ—struck a responsive chord.

Stephen Spender attempted to account for the widening interest in Edith's poetry by distinguishing between her early and later work. Admitting that he was a devotee of virtually all she had ever written, that much of his own earliest efforts were imitations of her work, Spender still maintained that it was mainly in Edith's later poems, her "prodigious hymns," that "the whole inner personality of the poet and a lifetime of experience" could be found.[15] He especially admired the imagery and music in Edith's mature work. Like a painter who uses very simple colors, she had made her images glow. Like a composer, she had made excellent use of the intervals and of notes widely separated one from the other. And it was through this combination of imagery and music, Spender believed, that Edith attained "the greatest intensity and clarity of purpose."[16]

Of Greater Importance

Early in 1943, Edith was riding the crest of critical acclaim. The Sitwell name once again had emerged from a literary limbo. The obscurity and decline Edith, Osbert, and Sacheverell suffered during the thirties was over. To celebrate, they decided upon a public poetry reading. On the one hand, with a reading they could help keep the arts alive during the war; on the other, they could consolidate their present position. Careful not to hog the limelight, they invited the leading poets in Britain to participate in the readings; and to make certain that all went well even rehearsed those in need of a bit of rehearsing.

The grand event took place on 14 April in Aeolian Hall, London, where *Facade* had been presented twenty years before. Of greater importance to Osbert and Edith was that the queen, Princess Elizabeth, and Princess Margaret were to be the honored guests. Beatrice Lillie had agreed to serve as program director, and to avoid conflicts of pride, the chosen poets would perform in alphabetical order. Edmund Blunden, Gordon Bottomly, Hilda Doolittle, T. S. Eliot, Walter de la Mare, and John Masefield, accordingly, were the first to read. Vita Sackville-West, Edith, Osbert, W. J. Turner, and Arthur Waley were chief among those reserved for the latter half of the program.

Unfortunately, all did not go as planned. As Edith wrote to Sacheverell—who for several reasons did not participate—there were nasty diversions, the most notorious of which concerned Lady Dorothy Wellesley's imbibing too much and, thinking she was whack-

ing Osbert with her walking stick, actually struck at Harold
Nicholson. Beatrice Lillie and Stephen Spender had to topple Lady
Dorothy to the ground in order to restrain her. [17] Obviously the press
was delighted, and such diversions—not the actual readings—drew
more attention to Edith and Osbert than they really desired.

Though ever loyal to his brother and sister, Sacheverell had no
regrets over missing the poetry readings. He could have been excused
from his duties with the Home Guard in Northamptonshire, but
he did not attend mainly because he was caught up in correcting
the proofs of his latest book, *Splendours and Miseries*. When Edith
read the work she readily agreed that Sacheverell had been wise to
concentrate his energy on a volume that she designated "one of the
greatest books written in our time." [18] Less enthusiastic than Edith,
most critics still ranked *Splendours and Miseries* among Sacheverells's
better books. John Lehmann, for one, wrote of it as "a masterpiece
in a prose genre" that Sacheverell had made peculiarly his own. [19]
Of even greater importance to Sacheverell than such acclaim was
the fact tht *Splendours and Miseries* ran through five printings.

Basically, *Splendours and Miseries* resembles many other volumes
that Sacheverell had written, being mainly a collection of personal
impressions and rhapsodical meditations. Its sections lack an overall
design, albeit certain essays do counterpoint others. Chief among
the "splendours" discussed are drawings of Fuseli, frescoes by Be-
nozzo Gozzoli in the Campo Santo at Pisa, Bruegel's phantasmagoric
paintings of Dulle Griet, and several fantasies on musical themes.
Among the "miseries" can be found such diverse essays as those on
the seventeenth-century mad messiah Sabbathai Zeni, a twentieth-
century's woman's poisoning of her lover, the starving dead of Ath-
ens under Nazi occupation, and even an imaginary tank battle on
the steppes of Russia.

Recollections of childhood and the love between himself and his
mother bring the book to a close. In his final chapter, "Songs My
Mother Taught Me," Sacheverell depicted Lady Ida in tender lyrical
terms. What he remembered best about his mother was that she
had "a wonderful way of carrying herself"; that she was "tall and
thin, and dark and beautiful"; that she had "a straight Grecian nose,
small mouth, dark brown eyes and little shell-like ears, set close to
her head . . . a straight thin neck . . . exquisite in its pose upon
her shoulders." [20]

Unlike Sacheverell, Edith did not reverence the memory of Lady Ida. Reading Sacheverell's endearing words about their mother disturbed Edith deeply. His "Songs My Mother Taught Me" opened old wounds. For several years Edith had allowed her lack of affection for her mother to fester to the point where she often spoke bitterly about her. After Lady Ida's death in 1937, Edith attempted to master her emotions. Not wishing "to be cruel about a poor dead woman," as she put it, Edith confessed to feeling pity for "a young creature, married against her will into a kind of slave-bondage to an equally unfortunate and pitiable man" (*TC*, 7). And about the same time that Edith was trying desperately to forgive her mother—and father—Sir George passed away. His death in 1943 further exacerbated Edith's pain and guilt.

In time, Edith came to realize that it was unreaonable to charge Sir George and Lady Ida with not giving her all the love and attention every child expects to receive from its parents. That she had often been an exasperating child, she could not deny; still, was her obstinate behavior reason enough for her parents to withhold their love? Perhaps, she feared, she would never find a proper explanation, especially since Sir George and Lady Ida often bestowed their affection upon Osbert and Sacheverell. But then she learned that Osbert had completed the first volume of his autobiography. Possibly with his objective and analytical skill Osbert had put family matters into proper perspective.

An Individual's Own Will

All during 1944, after publishing yet another volume of assorted essays, *Sing High! Sing Low!*, Osbert concentrated on his autobiography—a work that over the next six years ran into five volumes containing more than a half million words. The first volume he had originally entitled *The Cruel Month*: but then, having a mild interest in chiromancy, he decided to call it *Left Hand, Right Hand*, from the belief of palmists that the left hand reveals characteristics and events determined by birth, while the right shows those determined by an individual's own will. As he explained in a long introduction, he first started his autobiography to scrutinize the conflict between the two streams in his own life. In the process, he wove an entire era into a brilliantly composed and detailed tapestry.

In his introduction Osbert took care to note that the whole of experience seems to blur and dissolve before our very eyes. This being so, he felt a compulsion to record his dominant impressions in order to bring them once again into focus. Of necessity, he would be exact—and extravagant. "I want this work," he wrote of *Left Hand, Right Hand*, to be "full of detail, massed or individual, to be gothic, complicated in surface and crowned with turrets and with pinnacles . . . (*LH*, x). As a consequence, his autobiography would have to be full of others besides himself, his sister and brother; full of scenes and divertissements and individuals of every sort.

To effect a portrait of his age, to show how a child of his family should have developed—as well as how he actually did—would be his chief objectives. And having a preference for fantasy in art, and art in life, he would avoid as much as possible such mundane subjects as politics, commercialism, and technology. *Left Hand, Right Hand*, moreover, should primarily beguile a reader, not necessarily uplift his emotions or improve his mind: "I do not pretend to tell . . . everything, only to paint . . . in a setting, a portrait, of which, as in a surrealist picture, many diverse incidents compose the features. I leave the skeletons in their cupboards . . ." (*LH*, ix).

Dominating the narrative are two figures: Osbert's own self-portrait; and, illuminated by wit and affectionate understanding, Sir George gazing back toward a secure and distant past. Many pages, accordingly, are given over to the Sitwell family. Among ancestral kinsmen, Osbert finds traces of genius, bizarre and less apparent in Sir George than in his gifted children.

Osbert, ever mindful of how Edith had been troubled by Sacheverell's affective portrait of Lady Ida in *Splendours and Miseries*, managed to write about their mother with requisite circumspection. His own memory of Lady Ida was closer to that of Sacheverell's than to that of Edith's; and yet, without betraying his own vision of Lady Ida, Osbert recorded his, Edith's, and Sacheverell's childhood in such a way that he told the truth and managed to assuage Edith. Osbert's scenarios of their early life vis-à-vis Lady Ida and Sir George so impressed Edith that, when she mentioned *Left Hand, Right Hand* in a letter to Stephen Spender, she gushed: "In this wonderful book, I feel that something has been made of my parents' useless lives. And I remember that I shall never see them again. And that I am intensely proud of the book."[21]

As for his elder sister, Osbert remembered Edith best as a remarkably precocious child, a bit too much for her parents: "They mistook her nervous sensibility for awkwardness, imagination for falsehood, and a capacity for throwing the cloak of drama over everyday events—often the sign of an artist—for 'being affected' " (*LH*, 90). And then, as she grew older, instead of allowing her to find her own range, "they tried to force her to comply with their own measurements" (*LH*, 90). Sir George and Lady Ida were much better attuned to Sacheverell; for, understandably, as Osbert remembered him, he was always a particularly fascinating and genial child, possessed from his earliest days with an intense love of life and people. Sacheverell's love of life and his innate curiosity about others, Osbert concluded, "was undoubtedly the root of my brother's subsequent search for knowledge, and perpetual eagerness to know the ways of humanity in every part of the world" (*LH*, 165).

What action there is in *Left Hand, Right Hand*, apart from the interplay of its main characters, occurs in one of three places: Renishaw, the ancestral Sitwell estate; Scarborough, the town of Osbert's childhood; and the Castello di Montefugoni—once the seat of the Acciaiuoli family, Tuscan bankers and allies of the Medici—that Sir George acquired in 1908. But Osbert's life had many centers, aesthetic, emotional, and intellectual. Detailed within concentric orbits are his earliest familial experiences, his days in the military, his beginnings as an author. Like Proust, whom Osbert read religiously and replicated in his own way, he turned a microscope on recollected experiences to fathom essence and existence.

When published in 1945, *Left Hand, Right Hand* took the literary world by storm. Osbert was convinced that it was the best book of the twenty or so works he had written. Critics and readers concurred that the first volume of his autobiography was a beautiful and fascinating book, a veritable triumph, a masterpiece. The enthusiastic reception accorded *Left Hand, Right Hand* was exactly what Osbert in this period of his life most required. "I need praise as a salamander needs flame", he confessed to an acquaintance. [22]

If a display of genius requires the confluence of the man and the moment, as Matthew Arnold held, then *Left Hand, Right Hand*, coming as it did with the defeat of Germany, could not have been better timed. With sanity returning to the world, readers jaded by the bitter drama of total war were ready for Osbert's majestic autobiography. As John Pearson put it: "The very breath and detail of the book were in its favour. The verbally deprived could gorge themselves upon . . . convoluted prose, and relish the extravagance

with which he re-created a suddenly familiar world which everyone
had lost."[23]

Pain and Suffering

With the coming of peace in May 1945, Osbert and Edith began
to take stock of their years of retreat at Renishaw. Each had reacted
to the war differently. Osbert, for the most part, had put it out of
his mind mainly by re-creating the past. Had he not done so, he
would not have written *Left Hand, Right Hand*. Edith, on the con-
trary, had found it impossible to close her mind to the pain and
suffering the war had inflicted on countless millions. And had it
not been for her empathy, she would never have written her wartime
poetry.

In 1942, speaking for those without a voice, she had written her
Street Songs. Two years later, she completed her second volume of
war poetry, *Green Song and Other Poems*, a collection of sixteen poems
that rhapsodize her love for suffering humanity. The "green" of her
title had its origin in the poem "Green Flows the River Lethe-O,"
the river in which all bitter memories had to be submerged. In
1945, Edith completed her third volume of war poetry, *The Song
of the Cold*, an anthology of her best poems drawn from *Street Songs*
and *Green Song*, together with a few recent works she had contributed
to various periodicals and a small selection from earlier works.

Putting *Song of the Cold* together was not a difficult task, but
writing its title poem proved to be extremely trying. The horrors
of war had affected Edith so deeply that several times she had to
put aside her "Song of the Cold." In a personal note to John Lehmann
she tried to account for her creative problem. "I hurled myself on
it like a maniac, biting, tearing, kneading it into shape, and doing
what I can only describe as a blood transfusion act," she wrote.[24]
Often the most severe critic of her own work, in this case the agony
of gestation was worthwhile. After Edith finally got "Song of the
Cold" to read the way she knew it had to read, she announced:
"*Now* I am satisfied . . . and I like it."[25]

What she especially liked about her "Song of Cold" was the way
the "cold" eventually came to symbolize the hearts of humanity no
longer responsive to the warmth of nature.

> . . . these of the extinct faces
> Are a lost civilization, and have no possession

> But the night and day, those centuries of cold.
> Even their tears are changed now to the old
> Eternal nights of ice round the loveless head
> Of those who are lone and sexless as the Dead.

The "cold" of modern man, a consequence of egoism, greed, and selfishness, brings only death to the soul. To the all important question, "What life, what solar system of the heart / Could bring a restitution / To those who die of the cold?" she responded personally and didactically:

> Like the terrible leaves from the bough in the
>   violent spring . . .
> I am walking fire, I am all leaves—
> I will cry to the Spring to give me the birds' and the
>   serpents' speech
> That I may weep for those who die of the cold—
> The ultimate cold within the heart of Man.

Even after the armistice had been signed, Edith continued to compose poems concerned with man's terrible inhumanity to man. She could not drown her memories in the "River Lethe-O." It was as though, as Alan Ross put it, "her heart began to beat more in time with the world's heart."[26] The dropping of the atomic bomb over Hiroshima moved Edith to write her impassioned *Three Poems of the Atomic Age*—"Dirge for the New Sunrise," "The Canticle of the Rose," and "The Shadow of Cain."

Edith's atomic age poems came into being on 10 September 1945 when she and Osbert were on a train going to Brighton, where they were to give a reading. Glancing through the London *Times*, Osbert came across an eyewitness description of the actual dropping of the bomb. He began to read the account to Edith. What had most impressed the witness was that "a totem pole of dust . . . arose to the sun as testimony to the murder of mankind. . . . A totem pole, the symbol of creation, the symbol of generation" (*TC*, 181–82). At first, shocked by the image, Edith could not blot it out of her mind's eye; then, suddenly, countless lines of verse flooded into her head.

The first lines Edith put to paper several months later became the opening lines of "Dirge for the New Sunrise," subtitled "Fifteen

Minutes Past Eight O'Clock, on the Morning of Monday, the 6th
of August, 1945":

> Bound to my heart as Ixion to the wheel,
> Nailed to my heart as the Thief upon the Cross,
> I hang between our Christ and the gap where the
>   World was lost.

The rest of the poem is a vivid impression of her revulsion of what
happened at Hiroshima. The penury of man's spirit had made such
horror possible:

> —The ghost of the heart of Man . . . red Cain
> And the more murderous brain
> Of man, still redder Nero that conceived the death
> Of his mother Earth, and tore
> Her womb, to know the place where he was conceived.

Still, "no eyes grieved— / For none were left for tears."

In "The Canticle of the Rose," the personified Rose speaks of its
"pomegranate splendours . . . the ruby, garnet, almadine / Dews"
in whom "Christ's wounds . . . shine." Man, like the Rose, was
created to derive life from Light; but the "Shade of Man . . . Buyers
and Sellers cry / 'Speak not the name of Light.' " Evil men deny
the Light of the Sun and become "polarized to the dark / Earth-
center."

> But high upon the wall
> The Rose where the wounds of Christ are red
> Cries to the Light
> "See how I rise upon my stem, ineffable bright
> Effluence of bright essences. . . . From my little span
> I cry of Christ, Who is the ultimate Fire
> Who will burn away the cold in the heart of Man. . . ."

In "The Shadow of Cain" Edith again made good use of Light,
the creative power of Love as found in Nature and graced by Christ.
Interestingly, some of the best lines in the poem came to her in a
dream. The blasts over Hiroshima were

>   great lightenings
> In flashes coming to us over the floor:

> The Whiteness of the Bread—
> The Whiteness of the Dead—
> The Whiteness of the Claw—
> All this coming to us in flashes through
>   the open door.

The three flashes of lightning that she dreamed of, she believed, represented the primal realities of preservation, death, and struggle. Beyond the open door she visualized spring returning, and there would be "the grandeur of the Sun and Christ returning with the life-giving wheat of harvest." (*TC*, 183):

> And Everywhere
> The great voice of the Sun in sap and bud
> Fed from the heart of Being, the panic Power,
> The sacred Fury, shouts of Eternity,
> To the blind eyes, the heat in the wingèd seed,
>   the fire in the blood. . . .

Then came the horror, the symbol of which was seen by that eye-witness at Hiroshima:

> We did not heed the Cloud in the Heavens shaped
>   like the hand
> Of Man . . .
>   . . . the Primal Matter
> Was broken, the womb from which all life began.
> Then to the murdered Sun a totem pole of dust
>   arose in memory of Man.

A gulf was torn across the world, stretching its jaws from one end of the earth to the other. Loud were the cries in the hollow from those who once were men; and yet

> Those ashes that were men
> Will rise again
> To be our Fires upon Judgment Day!
> —who dreamed that Christ has died in vain?
> He walks again on the Seas of Blood, He comes
>   in the terrible rain.

Chapter Ten
Lionized at Last
Without Dejection or Despair

During the closing years of the forties, the Sitwells began to be lionized as one of the greatest literary families in the history of English letters. They had come a long way from the days in 1922 when they first drew considerable attention to themselves with *Facade*. Even their most captious critics had to concede that Edith, Osbert, and Sacheverell were now mature writers who, through the writing of more than a hundred volumes of poetry, fiction, biography, and history, had earned an enviable reputation as gifted, original, prescient authors.

Edith's latest poems, especially those in *The Song of the Cold, The Canticle of the Rose,* and *The Shadow of Cain,* were such that Kenneth Clark read them as masterpieces that restored belief in the human heart. So impressed was he with the metaphysical dimensions of her wartime poetry, the fact that Edith had evolved into a metaphysical poet, that Clark was moved to comment that one of her greatest achievements was to write for a suffering generation—and to do so without dejection or despair. "She is growing in power and confidence," he wrote, "so that we wait thirstily for each new poem, which, by its beauty, its compassion and its belief in the eternal process of recreation, can help us to endure the world's fever."[1]

Clark was far more interested in Edith's poetry than in Osbert's prose, but other critics began to refer glowingly to his *Left Hand, Right Hand* L.P. Hartley, for one, lauded Osbert's autobiography as "a work of tremendous complexity and subtlety . . . for which it is difficult to find an analogy in literature."[2] Hartley, fascinated by the work, did an analysis of *Left Hand, Right Hand,* as well as of the sequels that Osbert completed over the next five years.

The second volume of Osbert's remembrance of things past, *The Scarlet Tree,* published in 1946, focused on his days at Eton and his first sojourn in Italy under the tutoring control of Sir George. Hartley thought it as good as *Left Hand, Right Hand.* The London

Sunday Times considered it worthy of a prize of a thousand pounds and a commemorative gold medal. Nor were the critics disappointed with Osbert's third volume published two years later. In *Great Morning* he wrote in generous detail of his early days at Renishaw, his family's acquisition of Montefugoni, and his stressful military career.

Readers who delighted in the first three volumes of Osbert's ever-expanding autobiography, who were fascinated by his evocation of a civilization not far removed in time but nevertheless gone forever, took eagerly to *Laughter in the Next Room*. In this fourth volume, published in 1949, Osbert covered World War I, the twenties, and Sir George in his dotage. The following year Osbert concluded his autobiographical series with *Noble Essences: A Book of Characters*. This fifth volume is devoted to the importance of art in life and to reminiscences of his talented friends, the most prominent being Sir Edmund Gosse, Ronald Firbank, Gabrielle D'Annunzio, Ada Leverson, Rex Whistler, and Arnold Bennett.

Osbert and Edith were now at center stage, but Sacheverell, ever the modest intellectual, stood off to one side. Edith was concerned that he might have felt slighted or underrated. Sacheverell, however, never expressed envy of his brother or sister or of the many accolades they had received. Edith and Osbert, for example, had been made Fellows of the Royal Society of Literature; Sacheverell was not. Fortunately, Sacheverell's temperament was such that he preferred to avoid the limelight. All he wanted was time to concentrate upon the kind of books he liked to research and write. That he did not receive as much critical acclaim as Edith and Osbert were now receiving troubled him now and again; still, he took comfort from the highly favorable reception his *Splendours and Miseries* had received in 1943. The four volumes he completed in the late forties, unfortunately, did not merit the same attention.

One of his books, *British Architects and Craftsmen*, nevertheless, when published in 1945, did run into four printings. His next book, *The Hunters and the Hunted*, published in 1947, also had a moderate appeal. The *Spectator* described it as a wonderful study of "Byzantine mosaics, Picasso, Mozart, Venice . . . falcons, birds of paradise, huntsmen, hounds and many other things that tumble in front of the reader in a fine profusion."[3] The following year, Sacheverell completed two more books: another travel book, *The Netherlands*, and a series of impressions entitled *Noon and Night in London*.

In 1948, there was also a reprint of his *Collected Poems*, first published in 1936.

This time the critics were more laudatory than they had been a dozen years before. All 3,000 copies of *Collected Poems: Sacheverell Sitwell* sold, but the volume did little to enhance its author's reputation as a poet—despite several rave reviews. An enthusiastic critic for the *Times Literary Supplement* went so far as to declare that Sacheverell's *Collected Poems* deserved a wide public, that the publication proclaimed a poet of major significance. "From the work in this volume alone," he affirmed "there can be little doubt that posterity will find a place for him."[4]

In the light of such praise, Sacheverell joined Edith and Osbert at one and another of their readings. The Sitwells seemed a remarkably united family. Not until Osbert and Edith sailed off to the states in October 1948 without Sacheverell did a bit of ill-wind surface. When Evelyn Waugh, who was in New York at the time, ran into Osbert and Edith, he politely inquired: "Is Sachie joining you?" Their reply: "Alas, Sachie is High Sheriff of his county and therefore unable to leave the United Kingdom."[5] Sacheverell, it was apparent to Waugh, could easily have had an under-sheriff fill his sinecural position for a short time.

Edith tried to give the impression that she and her brothers were as close to one another as they had ever been. The truth was that the Sitwells were no different from many other families. Osbert, it seems, had first become aggrieved when Sacheverell broke up their close relationship to marry Georgia Doble; and then, over the years, misunderstandings accumulated to the point where Sacheverell was disturbed by Osbert's avuncular attitude toward him and his wife. Through it all, Edith did her best to remain neutral; yet when an opportunity came for her and Osbert to visit the states, she took it, even though it meant Sacheverell had to be left behind.

One of Osbert's explanations for not including Sacheverell had a ring of truth: "Three is one too many for lectures"; but the other, that he had "to underwrite the financial position of the lectures" and could not do so with three people, rung hollow.[6] There was every indication that lecturing and giving readings in the states would prove financially rewarding—and Sacheverell was in serious need of additional income. Then, too, Osbert had invited David Horner to go along—undoubtedly at Osbert's expense. Finally, playing the part of a benevolent brother, Osbert resolved that being left behind would be good for Sacheverell: he would have "to settle down and work"; and, as for his wife, she too would have "to settle down and learn how to manage his affairs for him."[7]

In the States

Crossing the Atlantic on the *Queen Mary* should have been an enjoyable experience, but it proved not to be for Osbert, Edith, or David Horner. Edith found the voyage exhausting, and Osbert and David grumbled about everything aboard the ship. Once they landed in New York, everything changed. Like most European visitors to the states, they anticipated the hustle and bustle of New York and were not disappointed. When Edith recorded her initial impression of America, she wrote: "Everybody seemed so young. It was not possible that people so alive could be so old" (*TC*, 210).

Edith, and Osbert settled into a comfortable suite in the St. Regis Hotel. They loved the hotel and everything about New York. They delighted in seeing old friends and meeting famous personalities. Foremost among friends for Edith was Pavel Tchelitchew, whom she had not seen in ten years. During the decade they were apart, they had exchanged countless letters, their correspondence serving both as outlet and solace. Pavel, having established himself in the states, awoke one day to find himself famous: the Museum of Modern Art purchased his monumental canvas *Hide and Seek*. In several letters to Edith, he had written of this canvas, its conception and execution, and how much he looked forward to having Edith stand beside him and soak in the beauty of his masterpiece.

One of the first things Pavel and Edith did, accordingly, was to visit his *Hide and Seek*. Edith did not know how to react when she first gazed upon its mass of embryonic shapes interlaced with hundreds of red and blue veins. Fearful of saying something inappropriate to the ultrasensitive artist, Edith said little; but Pavel, who had expected an enthusiastic response, could not understand that Edith's silence was actually a tribute to his art. The next day, when Edith put her thoughts about *Hide and Seek* on paper and sent them to Pavel, her gushing words of praise could not atone for the hurt Pavel had initially experienced. Their reunion was off to a bad start—and would get worse.

Edith and Tchelitchew could not communicate in person as well as they had through their letters. In addition, the artist was unconsciously jealous of Edith's reception in the states; and, on her part, Edith sensed their relationship was in its death throes. Fortunately, Edith's personal disappointments were more than compensated for by her public triumphs. Everywhere she and Osbert went they were enthusiastically welcomed. Waugh summed up their social and literary victories in a letter home to his wife: "The Sitwells are rampaging about New York cutting a terrific splash. . . ."[8] And in a note to Nancy Mitford, Waugh added that Osbert and Edith were "having one hell of a time. Every magazine has six pages of them headed 'The Fabulous Sitwells.' . . . Goodness how they are enjoying it."[9]

Osbert and Edith gave public recitals, lectured at dozens of universities, and spoke before diverse groups. Over ten thousand poetry lovers filled New York's Town Hall to attend a Sitwell reading. Their greatest triumph came at the performance of *Facade* at the Museum of Modern Art; those fortunate to be in the audience were ecstatic and reverential. Harold Acton did not exaggerate in the least when he stated: "The Sitwells were welcomed in America as few poets have been in England."[10]

Famous personalities lined up to meet Edith and Osbert, including Charlie Chaplin and Greta Garbo. At a literary party given at the Gotham Book Mart the Sitwells, reigning like royalty, received obeisance from Horace Greely, Gore Vidal, Tennessee Williams, Marianne Moore, Randal Jarrell, Delmore Schwartz, and other writers who had been summoned to meet Osbert and Edith. Needless to add, perhaps, the Sitwells enjoyed every glorious moment. Long before they returned to England Osbert and Edith knew they would visit the states again.

In 1950, they did so. This time they decided to take in the West Coast, meet motion picture stars, and allow the stars to meet them. Hollywood and its celebrities so impressed Edith that later she gave it a full chapter in her autobiography, writing of meeting such luminaries as Ethel Barrymore, Mary Pickford, Merle Oberon, and Marilyn Monroe. But there was also serious business to be discussed in Hollywood with the famous director George Cukor, who wanted to film Edith's *Fanfare for Elizabeth*, a biography of England's great queen that had been published in 1946.

Like most of Edith's prose works, *Fanfare for Elizabeth* had been written mainly for money. Neither authentic biography nor valid history, the book nevertheless became a best-seller; hence, Cukor's interest. In an honest moment, Edith admitted that *Fanfare for Elizabeth* had serious limitations. "It is a terrible book," she wrote of her meretricious labor; then added, "Well it is *all right* you know, but I am *not* a prose writer. I am a poet."[11]

Beyond the monetary reasons for writing *Fanfare for Elizabeth*, all her life Edith had a great affinity for the Virgin Queen. Edith delighted to recall that they were born on the same day—7 September—and had fathers who either ignored or mistreated them, mothers who were beautiful and capricious. In addition, Edith liked to think that she and Elizabeth both had unhappy youths, shared feelings of intrinsic greatness, and were convinced that they had destinies to fulfill. In writing about the travails of Elizabeth, Edith was obviously giving vent to her own deepest feelings. "It is this kinship between her subject and herself," Max Wykes-Joyce recognized "that makes Edith Sitwell's study of Elizabeth Tudor so much more moving a work than her *Victoria of England*."[12]

Fanfare for Elizabeth paints an excellent picture of sixteenth-century England. The licentiousness, grime, and intrigue of Henry VIII's court are depicted in detail. More attention is given to Henry and his court, in fact, than to Elizabeth. Early on she is introduced as "a sad little girl . . . in a world that would never understand her."[13] In her teens she comes to realize that she is a misunderstood, neglected, too-articulate princess born into "a Sophoclean tragedy of passions, faiths, lusts, ambition that had the fever of lust. . . ."[14] Uncertain whether she was in favor or about to be disinherited, Elizabeth continually felt the cruel indifference of first one stepmother, Jane Seymour, and then another, Katherine Howard.

The fanfare surrounding Elizabeth is at times difficult for the reader to follow; but then even the chief protagonists—who for the most part were crafty dissemblers and vicious liars—were not always sure themselves of what was happening. The rich and fanciful language Edith employed also tends to distract the reader's attention from the direction toward which events inevitably move. Many matters, furthermore, are left unresolved. To judge *Fanfare for Elizabeth* as a work of research and scholarship would of course be a mistake, for Edith's purpose was not orthodox biography but a dramatic re-creation of her subject's early history as seen through Edith's own powerful, identifying imagination. In addition *Fanfare for Elizabeth* is not the full story of a princess's life inasmuch as it treats Elizabeth only up to her fifteenth year: "The Great, the terrible tomorrow had not yet invaded her heart."

All the above having been said, George Cukor still believed that *Fanfare for Elizabeth* would make a good screenplay. In spite of every effort on his part, however, the film did not get under way. One of the chief reasons was the difficulty of fitting Edith's concept of Elizabeth into a Hollywood mold; another, just as valid, was fitting Charles Laughton into the role of Henry. As conceived by Edith, Henry VIII was "a man of great personal beauty . . . of great magnificence and power . . . the prince with the face of an angel who had fallen under the spell of his own princely will."[16]

When all seemed doomed to failure, Cukor in a letter to Edith noted that he had been put into "a flurry of excitement by a cable from the Oliviers.[17] Vivien Leigh had written that she had read Edith's script and was anxious to play Anne Boleyn. The only problem, she added, was that "Larry is now so concentrating on Richard [III] that I doubt if anything else would really interest him at the moment."[18] Cukor entertained hopes that Olivier could be won over, nevertheless, and he notified Edith that the studio would go ahead as soon as the Oliviers were under contract. As things turned out, Cukor's optimism proved unjustified. All plans for filming *Fanfarfe for Elizabeth* had to be abandoned.

A Matter of Degrees

Edith's lack of success with *Fanfare for Elizabeth* in Hollywood dismayed her greatly, but only for a short time. So many other wonderful things were happening about her that she soon forgot her movie script and all the problems it had caused her. In 1949, for example, she had been named an Honorary Associate of the American Institute of Arts and Letters. Then, in 1951, Oxford University conferred upon her a Doctor of Letters degree. The only other woman with an honorary doctorate from Oxford, Edith soon learned, was the queen. Edith could also boast of two other honorary degrees: one from Leeds, that had been awarded in 1947; the other, from Durham, awarded in 1949. A fourth honorary degree from Sheffield University followed a few years later.

Edith loved to call herself *Dr.* Sitwell, and usually demanded that others do likewise—until 1954, that is, when she was created a Dame Commander of the Order of the British Empire; thereafter she had to be addressed as *Dame* Edith. Never before had a female poet been so honored, and congratulations flowed in from all sides. Edith especially valued Eliot's personal letter of felicitation. "I was very happy," he wrote, "that the sovereign had recognized the judgment of the world of letters and conferred an honour . . . which will give pleasure to your friends and satisfaction to your admirers. . . ."[19] Compton Mackenzie's public acknowledgment of the signal honor Queen Elizabeth II had bestowed upon Edith was also gratifying. "Dr. Edith Sitwell is the greatest poet that the women of England have yet produced," he wrote in the *Spectator*. "and the Order of the British Empire was beginning to look rather ridiculous on Parnassus without Dr. Sitwell as a Dame."[20]

The passage of years, it was obvious to Mackenzie, had given a rich maturity to Edith's work. This maturity was particularly apparent in a slim volume of her recent poetry, *Gardeners and Astronomers*, published in 1953. Several of the poems in *Gardeners and Astronomers* had previously been published in various magazines, journals, and newspapers, most of which welcomed anything she cared to submit.

Each of the fifteen poems in *Gardeners and Astronomers* is unique, but all are concerned with the timeless themes of the life cycle, the movement from birth and life to death and regeneration. In the vast impersonal order of nature, moreover, Edith had found personal meaning. Through a humane tenderness and merciless egotism man seemed both a victim and a conqueror, but in all her lines, despite occasional irony, can be found a sense of life's essential beauty. As for symbols, she drew them from classical myths and Christian legends, from the dawn of history and from contemporary affairs, with all subsumed under the universality of the sea, the sun, the stars. Just as the world of nature is transformed and restored by the creative action of the sun, she maintained, so too can love transform and heal all human suffering. Man is not born to quarrel with existence, but he must learn to accept life on its own terms.

Edith's acceptance of life on its own terms demanded a metaphysical approach. She had taken such an approach in 1929 when she pondered the sufferings of Christ in *Gold Coast Customs*: "the Starved Man hung upon the Cross, the God . . . who bears in his heart all wounds." Suffering thereafter became a dominant theme in several of her poems. In "Still Falls the Rain," in particular, she wrote about the slaughter of war in terms of the Crucifixion. Then she began to incorporate thoughts of the re-creating energy of divine love into her work, especially in "The Shadow of Cain."

Over a period of more than twenty years, ever so slowly, she had come to accept the tenets of orthodox Christianity, which can be ascertained from a chronological reading of her *Collected Poems* published in 1954. To allay any doubts, moreover, she noted in a long introduction to the volume that her time of experimentation was over, that she was reaching for ideals, that she had come to bless Christ and his people. Spiritually, she had arrived at that point in her life when she yearned "to give holiness to each common day," to write poems that would be "hymns of praise to the glory of life."[21]

In April 1955, at the age of sixty-seven, Edith converted to Roman Catholicism. Becoming Roman Catholic she hoped would give her a sense of security and happiness. To a certain extent, she had been influenced by friends and acquaintances, among them Evelyn Waugh, Graham Greene, Roy Campbell, Alec Guiness, David Horner, Father Martin D' Arcy, and Father Philip Caraman. There also was the prime example of T. S. Eliot, who had joined the Anglican church.

Alluding to spiritual matters in her poetry was one thing, but discussing her personal religious beliefs was another. Edith, accordingly, seldom spoke of her conversion with others; but the impression they received was that her metanoia was both deep and lasting. Elizabeth Salter, who was her confidant and secretary from 1957 until Edith's death in 1964, once described Edith as "a natural Catholic." Not being a member of the Roman Catholic church, Elizabeth Salter hesitated to broach the subject of religion to Edith; still, she came to the conclusion that Edith's acceptance of the Catholic faith "represented not so much a change in outlook as the logical conclusion of a way of thought."[22]

One day, however, curiosity got the better of Salter and she inquired of Edith her reason for conversion. Edith responded simply that she had sought "the discipline, the fire, and the authority of the Church."[23] What Salter found of even more significance was Edith's admission that she had been greatly impressed by the simple faith that illuminated the faces of peasants she had witnessed praying in small Italian churches. At first, Edith continued, she felt unworthy of such a faith. This humility, which underlay the idiosyncrasies of her personality, seemed to Salter "to be the core of [Edith's] sincerity as a person, and as a poet."[24] Beneath the witty, ironic, capricious outer Edith was "the 'Sitwell soul' that stood in awe of the ultimate reality and remained uncorrupted before the mystery and miracle of life."[25]

Hopes and Praise

Both Father Caraman, who formally received Edith into the church, and Waugh, who served as her godfather, had hopes that Osbert and Sacheverell would follow their sister's example. Waugh recorded such sentiments in a letter to Edith when he wrote: "Is it exorbitant to hope that your example and prayers may bring Osbert to the Faith? I have often thought I saw in his writings (tho' not as plain as in yours) that he was near the truth."[26] Osbert had no objections to Edith's conversion; in fact, he encouraged her to do so. But Osbert was not prepared to take such a step himself; nor was Sacheverell the least bit inclined to follow Edith into the church.

Though wrong about Osbert's coming "near the truth," Waugh was correct in his assessment of Osbert's career. Osbert's autobiographical volumes, Waugh was convinced, had earned their author "a secure place in English literature."[27] All during the early fifties, Osbert was as prolific as he had ever been. In 1952, for example, he published *Wrack at Tidesend: A Book of Balnearics*, which he designated the second volume of his *England Reclaimed*. In the following year, Duckworth issued *The Collected Stories of Osbert Sitwell*. And he was busy writing essays and planning a postscript to his autobiography.

Waugh's finest tribute to Osbert appeared in the *Sunday Times* of 7 December 1952, the day after Osbert celebrated his sixtieth birthday. After praising his subject as "the tall, well-dressed figure" with "the courteous manner," Waugh went on to state that, within his experience, most writers were "dull dogs" who came alive only with pen in hand at ease behind their desks. Osbert proved an exception, always "a full, rich singular personality first, and a shelf of books second." As a writer with a personality, Osbert had "acquired his reputation first, then seriously settled down to earn it." His development continued into late middle age, Waugh stressed, so that Osbert's latest books were consistently his best.[28]

Few denied that Osbert deserved the homage Waugh heaped upon him. And just as Edith had reaped her share of individual honors, Osbert accumulated his in like measure. In 1946, to be specific, St. Andrews awarded him an honorary Doctor of Laws. In 1950, he was declared an Honorary Associate of the American Institute of Arts and Letters. In 1951, Sheffield University awarded him an honorary Doctor of Letters. Then, in 1952, being not only a successful author but also the fifth Sitwell baronet (having succeeded Sir George upon his death nine years before), Osbert was invited to join the queen mother in her box in Westminster Cathedral when Elizabeth II was crowned queen.

Four years later, in 1956, Osbert was made a Commander of the British Empire. He was pleased with the honor, but at the time Sacheverell protested privately to a friend that it was really "a measly decoration" to bestow on a major English writer, that in the eyes of the British government writers ranked far below politicians, military men, entertainers, and sportsmen.[29] Osbert, nonetheless, accepted his C.B.E. graciously; for, as he readily admitted, he thrived on honors and was never immune to flattery. In 1958, he was further honored when he was elevated to Companion of Honor.

Sacheverell, regrettably, was not the recipient of such awards, but he was always quick to commend Osbert or Edith whenever one of them added new luster to the Sitwell name. True, he had envied them their triumphs in the states, but he enjoyed a successful one-man lecture tour of America in the autumn of 1951. Though his impact was far less than that of Osbert and Edith, he handled himself well at centers on the East Coast, as well as in Houston, Chicago, Palm Beach, and Montreal.

During his time in America, Sacheverell was so busy preparing talks and readings, or spending time in transit and sightseeing, that he did not have the time to produce a book of his travels. Virtually every one of his previous trips to foreign lands had resulted in a volume or two; but, then, the states lacked an aesthetic tradition or matters that Sacheverell loved to write about, the unique art and architecture that he had found all over the Iberian Peninsula, for example. His visits to Spain and Portugal had resulted in two distinct books. In 1950, he published *Spain,* a descriptive guidebook to Andalucia, Castile, Aragon, Valencia, and Levante. Four years later, he published *Portugal and Madeira*, in which he dilated upon such things as hibiscus and oleander, organ cases and wine lodges, ruined abbeys and splendid cathedrals.

In 1956, Sacheverell published another travel book, *Denmark,* after his visit to that country a short while before. As was his custom, he focused on matters of primary interest to him, material not found in other guidebooks, and he wrote almost as much of castles and palaces as he did on the art treasures of the Danes. And then his travels through the Middle East resulted in another erudite book published in 1957, which he entitled *Arabesque and Honeycomb,* a connoisseur's guide to Teheran and Isfahan, Islamic art, sacred mosques, the ruins of Petra, and Christian sanctuaries in Jerusalem. In 1958, he collaborated with Tony Armstrong Jones on a study of Malta, in which the photographs of Jones take up almost one third of its 144 pages. The following year Sacheverell wrote the introduction to *Austria,* a volume of some 200 mostly full-page photographs taken by Toni Schneiders and meant to capture the geographic, human, and cultural features of that country.

In 1959, after an extended visit to Japan, Sacheverell published *Bridge of the Brocard Sash.* This discursive study offers provocative comments on the culture of a land that for several years had stimulated his imagination. It can be said, in fact, that Sacheverell reacted to the wonders of Japan in his maturity with the same enthusiasm that in his youth he had reacted to the grandeur of Italy. He wrote, accordingly, with gusto of the Japanese countryside, the gardens, theaters, art, and architecture of its people.

There seemed to be no limit to the number of countries Sacheverell might visit and the number of travel books he could churn out. Indeed, if prizes and awards were bestowed for sheer industry, Sacheverell would have garnered more honors than Edith and Osbert combined. It was not that he had a more facile pen; rather, he wrote many books because they were a primary source of income. In contrast to Edith, who had earned tidy sums with her prose studies, especially her filmscript for *Fanfare for Elizabeth,* and Osbert, who because of primogeniture could live the life of an aristocrat, Sacheverell had to labor over his books to support his wife and two children.

Sacheverell enjoyed writing his books, but evidence of his private pain may be found in his *Journey to the Ends of Time,* a cornucopia of curiosa, which he worked on all through the fifties and finally published in 1959. This volume echoes some of the deep pessimism that had already surfaced in *The Dance of The Quick and the Dead* and *Splendours and Miseries*. Subtitled *Lost in the Dark Wood*, this work can be read as an existential pilgrimage, a report of some of the disappointments and the distress that Sacheverell had experienced over his fifty years. One critic referred to the work as "an extraordinary achievement of time remembered, a magnificent collection of images, terrifying at times . . . which make up a poet's nostalgia for the grandeur and miseries of human existence."[30]

Outwardly, Sacheverell was a successful author, a gifted member of a famous literary family. Few men seemed so blest. While not so widely hailed as Edith or Osbert, in many ways he was more fortunate. Unlike Edith, whose relatiomship with Pavel Tchelitchew ended disastrously, Sacheverell had a wonderful marriage to Georgia Doble. Unlike Osbert, who was now entering the secondary stages of Parkinson's disease, Sacheverell was in moderately good health. But, regrettably, even if one has a good marriage and fair health there are countless other matters that can cause anguish, especially if one frets over what life should be—and seldom is. Undoubtedly sibling rivalry also played a role, though Sacheverell did not give expression to such in his intimate *Journey to the Ends of Time: Lost in the Dark Wood*.

Power and Glory

Toward the end of the fifties, Osbert, mainly because of poor health, was forced to slack off on his writing; but Edith, though she was moving up in years, completed another anthology. A massive volume of more than a thousand pages, her *Atlantic Book of British and American Poetry* was published in the United States in 1958, in England a year later. Critics in both countries justifiably pointed out deficiencies and omissions. She had allocated only three pages to Burns and but four to Browning, for example, though she allowed fourteen pages to Osbert and Sacheverell. To divert attention from the misjudgments many critics pointed out, Edith boasted that she was the first anthologist to represent such poets as John Clare and Yeats properly; moreover, that she had included "the most heavenly early religious poems—some unknown outside specialist anthologies, wonderful early love poems, Tudor poems, and Elizabethan and 17th-century poems."[31]

Compiling her *Atlantic Book of British and American Poetry* had kept Edith from her own creative work, but as soon as she completed the anthology she devoted most of her time to a sequel to *Fanfare for Elizabeth*. This new biography, a concurrent study of Elizabeth of England and Mary of Scotland, was entitled *The Queens and the Hive* to reflect Edith's view of both queens as bees, England a hive, and the honey of the hive the power and glory of all Britain.

That Edith wrote as a poet rather than a historian accounts for both the beauty and the weakness of this period piece. On the one hand, she attempted to be factually accurate; on the other, her chief concern was to develop the personalities of both queens, even if it meant emphasizing some matters more than others without a strict regard for relative historical importance. She therefore consulted all the requisite materials, but imaginatively interpreted several of her sources.

The Queens and the Hive paints a somber picture of England during the last year of Henry VIII and the brief reigns of Edward VI and Mary Tudor by way of prologue. A time of fire and blood, treachery seemed everywhere. The accession of Elizabeth at first was like a great clean wind. As queen, she ruled with the love of her subjects, her clever diplomacy granting England stability and peace. But Edith's brilliant imagery notwithstanding, Elizabeth is dimly drawn. Wherein lay her greatness—the central question that has fascinated all historians of the Tudor Age—Edith failed to answer. She did attempt to deal with several of the enigmas surrounding Elizabeth's life, however.

Edith notes, for example, that the queen's affection for Essex was not the love of a vain old woman for a handsome young man; rather, Elizabeth saw in him the son she might have borne. As for "Bloody Mary," Edith prefers to call her Mary I of England and to paint her as a good and virtuous woman. That Mary the Catholic pesecuted Protestants, Edith of course could not deny, but she reminds the reader that cruelty begets cruelty and that neither Catholic nor Protestant was free of guilt.

The portrait of Mary of Scotland is more vividly drawn than that of Mary of England or, indeed, of Elizabeth. Mary Queen of Scots being Catholic, Edith emphasized, made the rivalry between the two great queens much more deadly. In writing of both, Edith tried to be objective, but occasionally she tended to favor her own adopted Catholic faith. Scotland's John Knox is depicted as a gloomy, self-righteous figure; England's Edmund Campion, as a saintly Jesuit martyred for adherence to traditional religious truth. Captivated by Campion's martyrdom, Edith devoted almost as many pages to the event as she did to the greatest victory of Elizabeth's long reign, the defeat of the Spanish Armada.

Edith thought highly of *The Queens and the Hive* and judged it, as did most of its critics, far superior to *Fanfare for Elizabeth*. The fact that she dedicated the volume to George Cukor has certain implications. One was a simple gesture to commend him publicly for his unsuccessful efforts to turn *Fanfare for Elizabeth* into a Hollywood film; another, undoubtedly, was to call his attention to a far greater historical study that had all the ingredients for a truly outstanding cinematic production. Cukor, busy with a dozen other projects, did not rise to the bait. Fortunately for Edith, his apparent indifference was overshadowed by a combination of other favorable factors.

The year was 1962, and, in addition to the publication of *The Queens and the Hive*, her *Fanfare for Elizabeth* was reissued and had another good sale. *The Outcasts*, which was to be her last book of poems, was also published in the same year. Even more important than these three publications and their favorable reception was that Edith had reached her seventy-fifth year. After sixty years of dedication to literature, she was now at the pinnacle of her career. To celebrate her birthday, a Celebration Concert was organized by Sacheverell's son Francis and scheduled to be held at London's Royal Festival Hall on 9 October.

Edith was of course overjoyed to learn of the Celebration Concert, though she did her best to minimize the event. "The 9th should be a day for all present to remember," she quipped in a letter to Noel Coward, with whom she had recently reconciled after a period of forty years. "Never before has anyone attended their own Memorial Service."[32] In a letter to John Gielgud she echoed similar sentiments. The press are "mad with the excitement about my approaching demise," she wrote.[33] But she actually loved the fuss and excitement and was delighted when her old friend Cecil Beaton took pictures of her for publication in various newspapers and magazines.

The night of the concert provided a triumphal climax to Edith's lifelong dedication to literature. Present at her apotheosis were many of her closest friends and admirers: Sir Kenneth and Lady Clark, Sir

Charles and Lady Snow, Cyril Connolly, Harold Acton, Stephen Spender, and Father Caraman. A high proportion of those who packed the auditorium were young enthusiasts who knew Edith only from her works. Obviously, the entire Sitwell clan was present: Osbert, Sacheverell and his wife Georgia and their two sons, Francis and Reresby.

To lead things off, Edith read several of her recent poems. Peter Pears then sang Benjamin Britten's setting for "Still Falls the Rain." The English Chamber Orchestra brought the first part of the program to a close with Rossini's Sonata No. 1 in G and Mozart's Divertimento in D. The pièce de résistance of the evening was reserved for the second part of the program: a recitation of the twenty-one pieces of *Facade* delivered by Irene Worth and Sebastian Shaw to the perfectly matched music of Sir William Walton, who conducted the Chamber Orchestra.

The audience, as John Lehmann remembered the night, "seemed absolutely determined to give Edith a tremendous ovation," and all during the performance of *Facade* responded "to every turn of wit, every fantastic image and rhyme, with a low growl of laughter and delight."[34] *Facade*, over a span of forty years, had achieved the status of a classic. Those in the audience could not have been more appreciative. After wildly applauding the readers, the instrumentalists, and Sir William Walton, the three thousand members in the Royal Festival Hall turned as one to the box in which Edith was sitting and thunderously clapped and cheered for almost five minutes. Overcome, Edith waved and wept.

Winding Down

In the same year as Edith's Diamond Jubilee Celebration, Osbert published *Tales My Father Taught Me,* a postcript to his celebrated fivefold autobiographical sequence he had initiated in 1945 with *Left Hand, Right Hand. Tales My Father Taught Me* is a collection of twenty-eight anecdotes, which, for one reason or another, he had omitted from his previous five volumes, though several had been printed in the *Atlantic Monthly*, *Vogue*, and other periodicals. Most of the *Tales* are slight and Osbert, wisely, made no attempt to link them into a narrative. Each anecdote, instead, is its own evocation of the leisured eccentricities of a bygone aristocracy. Sir George is of course the key figure in Osbert's delightfully re-created microcosm.

Devotees of Osbert's monumental autobiography took to *Tales My Father Taught Me* as bees to nectar. A few critics, however, grumbled about Osbert's ornate prose. "At its most elaborate and elongated," Michael Holyroyd complained, "it reads like that of Sir Thomas Browne after being translated by Proust into French and subsequently rendered back into English by Henry James.[35] But Holyroyd had never favored the Sitwells, especially not Osbert, and he was less than objective in his comments on *Tales My Father Taught Me*. In similar fashion, Malcolm Muggeridge, who had skirmished with the Sitwells before, depreciated the *Tales*. Osbert's amusing stories about Sir George, Muggeridge found "really rather tedious."[36]

Osbert hardly enjoyed the barbs of captious critics, but, having a thicker skin than that of Edith, tended to ignore such cutting remarks. At his age—he was now seventy—he was virtually immune to unfavorable prattle about his books. He held himself fortunate in having been able to publish virtually everything he had written. Over the years, he had cultivated his own reading public, and his readers awaited his every book. In 1954, he gave them *The Four Continents: More Discussion on Travel, Art and Life*. In 1958, he published *On the Continent: A Book of Inquilinics,* another book of poetry, which he labeled the third volume of *England Reclaimed*. The following year there was his *Fee Fi Fo Fum: A Book of Fairy Stories*. And two years later, his publisher issued a selection of seven stories from his *Collected Stories* of 1953 under the title *A Place of One's Own and Other Stories*.

That Osbert completed as much as he did during the fifties is remarkable when his age and advanced Parkinson's disease are taken into account. The publication of *Pound Wise* in 1963 was to be his last book, a collection of some forty-six essays that had first appeared in the pages of magazines and newspapers. In subject matter, they range in mood from gentle vignettes of the last remnants of the Chinese aristocracy in Peking to nostalgic reflections on London, its inhabitants, its streets, and its fog. Not only do these short pieces have the world for locale, they cover almost a half century in time, from Edwardian days to the aftermath of World War II. Informative, sardonic, and incisive, they delve into such diverse subjects as "Games," "Dogs," "Private Schools," and "Rules for Being Rude." Entertaining, entrancing, and often infuriating, these last essays reveal the full range of Osbert's dazzling virtuosity in a genre where he had few equals.

About the same time that Osbert's last book was being published, Edith was working on what she knew was to be her last work. For several years she had given thought to writing her memoirs and realized the time to do so was short. Originally she planned to call the volume *More in Sorrow*, but she finally settled upon *Taken Care Of*. Her new title was not meant to connote, as is frequently charged, that she had *taken care of* her enemies, all those who had attacked her in one fashion or another, though it must be admitted that she did write unflatteringly of those she considered her chief foes. She had several nasty things to say about F. R. Leavis and Wyndham Lewis. Nor did she fail to slam D. H. Lawrence, who she believed parodied the entire Sitwell family in his *Lady Chatterly's Lover*. But to soften things a bit, she noted in her preface that she really meant to hurt no one. Those who she gave a few "hard slaps," she maintained, truly deserved them: "I have attacked nobody unless they first attacked me" (*TC*, vii).

What Edith took care of specifically are the important recollections of her early days, her aspirations as a poet, the inspirations for much that she had written, her multiple friendships—and most of the good and some of the bad she had experienced over the years. She had no desire to weave an elaborate, ornate, subtly composed tapestry to rival Osbert's autobiography. *Taken Care Of* is, instead, breezy, abrupt, tangential. At best, it is only a partial record of her life, ending with her days in Hollywood and revealing nothing of her conversion to Catholicism.

Nor did Edith cover her relationship with Tchelitchew. Aside from a few words about what a great artist he was, she had little to say about the only man she ever loved. She omitted any reference to the grief she felt when she first learned that Tchelitchew had died in Rome on 31 July 1957. Bitter about their love that was never meant to be, it took Edith several years to forgive the artist completely. In *Taken Care Of*, written seven years after Tchelitchew's death, when much of her pain had diminished, she stretched the truth considerably in claiming that he was "the most generous man I have ever known, a wonderful friend, and tireless in thinking of ways in which to help others" (*TC*, 162). The truth about their tempestuous relationship will not be known until their correspondence, which was deposited in a vault in the Yale University Library, is made available in the year 2000.

As for *Taken Care Of*, Edith knew that this would be her last book. She suspected that she was close to death; and, as things turned out, the volume, a pastiche of brilliant threads and banal patches, finally had to be assembled with scissors and paste and published posthumously. Osbert also suspected that *Pound Wise* would be his last work. Of necessity, both Edith and Osbert had begun to wind down in the sixties. Sacheverell, on the other hand, published two more books in 1961, *Golden Wall and Mirador: Travels and Observations in Peru* and *Great Houses of Europe*. But he, too, had been slowing down, for his next important work was not published until four years later. No longer could he produce a book or two a year.

In 1965, he published *Monks, Nuns and Monasteries*. Though this fascinating study gives no indication that he favored the cloistered life, he did discourse at length upon certain churches and works of religious art that the dedicated few enjoyed in various monasteries in England, France, Germany, Italy and Spain. Four years later he published *Gothic Europe*, a potpourri of description, comparison, analogy and personal reminiscences of the art and architecture of medieval England and the Continent. Then he devoted another four years to *For Want of a Golden City*, a continuation of his *Journey to th Ends of Time*. Once again, Sacheverell dwelt upon the golden dreams of his youth and the disappointments that followed as he tried to create his own palace of art.

Looking back on his long life, Sacheverell realized that though he had gone everywhere, seen and experienced at firsthand the world's greatest works of art, his dreams of attaining an Eldorado had all but evaporated. Faith in art had sustained his quest for almost eighty years, yet from *For Want of a Golden City* a reader would infer that Sacheverell's dedication to art for the sake of art was tenuous and quixotic. Nonetheless, in 1982, in his eighty-fifth year, he tried another volume of poetry, his sixteenth by actual count. *An Indian Summer,* a collection of 100 of his recent poems, is a brilliant brew of wisdom and melancholy, beauty and delight. Sacheverell was highly pleased that the *Spectator* in its 18 December 1982 issue selected it as one of the "Books of the Year."

Now, even though he is approaching ninety, Sacheverell is mentally alert and still creatively inclined. Indeed, a short while ago he noted in a letter that he was not fond of responding to questions about himself or his family. Since "one thing . . . leads to another," he really preferred to be "left alone and undisturbed" in order "to have the will and energy" to accomplish what he hopes still lies before him.[37] He prefers not to reveal what his next book may be.

Chapter Eleven

Epilogue

Any evaluation of the Sitwells has to take into account that as writers and personalities they were widely admired and narrowly detested. Those who disliked them believed they had good reasons for doing so, and they took every opportunity, so it seems, to discredit them publicly. F. R. Leavis, for one, dismissed Edith and her brothers as belonging "more to the history of publicity than poetry."[1] Malcolm Muggeridge, for another, openly complained that he had long been of the opinion that "the Sitwells, individually and collectively, were among the major bores of the age."[2]

Edith, being the most prominent and controversial of the trio, was the recipient of far more brickbats than those aimed at Osbert and Sacheverell. Geoffrey Grigson, who first sparred with Edith in 1930, allowed their feud to simmer for thirty-five years. Even after her *Taken Care Of* was published, posthumously, Grigson felt a need to even up the score. In a long review of her autobiography, he focused on what he considered its contumelious insults, its nastiness combined with triviality. In more than 2,000 words he attacked Edith's "sneering malice, megalomania, arrogance and . . . considerable stupidity," and in a final bit of overkill concluded that in everything she wrote she was "an amateur, a poseur of art."[3]

Much of the adverse criticism leveled against the Sitwells has been hyperbolic and ad hominem. Many highly favorable remarks about them likewise tend to be just as exaggerated and personal. Significantly, though often denounced, they could not be ignored. Virtually all they wrote was read avidly; yet they had few imitators. An identifiable Sitwell school never grew around them. Their uniqueness simply could not be duplicated; but, then, as Waugh once quipped: "Three of them was enough."[4]

The most prolific of literary families, the Sitwells were eclectic in their interests and in their tastes. They drew inspiration from the commedia dell'arte and the Ballets Russes, from Dickens and D'Annunzio, from Baudelaire and Rimbaud, from Claude and Marinetti, from the baroque and chinoiserie—all of which blended into their individual tapestries of creativity. They accomplished far more than did the Lambs (Charles and Mary), the Rossettis (Dante, Christina, and Michael), the Brontes (Emily, Charlotte, Anne, and Branwell), or the Michael Fields (Katherine Bradley and her niece Edith Cooper).

Waugh, one of the Sitwells' earliest and most faithful admirers, maintained that the trio served as models for himself and his literary classmates when he was an undergraduate at Oxford. Their work, he held, did not encourage slavish imitation as much as it served to provoke him and his friends to put their thoughts down on paper. The Sitwells were a stimulus more than a source for they always radiated "an aura of high spirits, elegance, impudence, unpredictability, above all sheer enjoyment. . . ." Waugh's supreme compliment he summed up in seven words: "They took the dullness out of literature."[5] To what extent they deserve the adulation of Waugh—or the strictures of such critics as Leavis, Muggeridge, and Grigson—makes for interesting debate, but few would deny that the Sitwells rest securely on a plateau far above midpoint in the hierarchy of twentieth-century literary figures.

The trajectories of the Sitwells' individual careers has already been covered in previous chapters, but by way of summation it may be well to recall that their reputations varied decade to decade. In the twenties they were in the vanguard of artistic experimentation, the center of spirited controversy. In the thirties, the pendulum swung the other way and a more socially concerned generation tended to think of them as irrelevant if not outmoded. But, then, during the period of World War II, Edith found her widest audience, principally because of her war poems, Osbert achieved wide acclaim for his autobiographical volumes, and Sacheverell's studies became standard fare for devotees of art and architecture.

In the 1950s, they reveled in being lionized on two continents. Edith and Osbert became the toast of New York and even conquered Hollywood. At the height of their fame, Edith and Osbert suffered a debilitation of health that brought on their deaths in the sixties. To state that the Sitwells were somewhat ignored during the seventies in no way diminishes their accomplishments; for they never wrote for the platitudinous multitude, being generally more concerned with reaching an elite, cultivated readership. Though there has been little scholarly interest in their work during the eighties, most of their best books are still in print[6] and presumably being read.

Edith's early experimental poetry, especially *Bucolic Comedies* and *The Sleeping Beauty*, stands up well. Her macabre masterpiece *Gold Coast Customs* deserves most of the praise it received. Her war verse, particularly *The Shadow of Cain, The Song of the Cold,* and *The Canticle of the Rose,* is still worthy of commendation. Chief among her prose works are *I Live under a Black Sun* and *The Queens and the Hive.*

What was especially important to Edith was that so many of her fellow poets, among them Yeats and Eliot, Dylan Thomas and Stephen Spender, spoke of her as one of the most creative artists of the century. Today admirers of her work rank the poems of her mature years higher than the verbal legerdemain of her experimental period. Louise Bogan, however, is one of the few who prefer Edith's earlier efforts to her later reflections on the world's evils.[7] That Edith was a master technician, an adroit inventor of rhythms and of rhymes to mark them percussively, is obvious to anyone familiar with *Facade*—the work that first brought her notoriety and still draws an abundant number of readers to her other works.

Her *Collected Poems* still finds a substantial audience, though individual readers are not as enthusiastic as was the late Cyril Connolly, who once wrote: "When we come to compare the collected poems of Dame Edith Sitwell with those of Yeats, or Eliot or . . . Auden it will be found that hers have the purest poetical content of them all."[8] Allen Tate tended to agree with Connolly, but he summed up Edith less extravagantly when, shortly after her death, he commented that she was "one of the great poets of the twentieth century . . . a remarkable and independent personality."[9]

Though Osbert early in his career longed to be a great poet, and achieved moderate success with his satirical *Argonaut and Juggernaut*, he wisely turned his attention to prose. Most of his short story collections deserve a second reading, especially *Triple Fugue*. To claim that his best novel, *Before the Bombardment*, has much of Dickens about it is high praise on the one hand but implies on the other that most of his fiction belongs more to the late nineteenth century, not with the best examples of the contemporary novel. Whatever may be the ultimate critical response to *The Man Who Lost Himself* and *Miracle on Sinai*, there is no denying that his real ability as an artist is most evident in the record of his own life. Despite the puff and presentation found throughout *Left Hand, Right Hand, The Scarlet Tree, Great Morning,* and *Laughter in the Next Room,* it is no exaggeration to propose that these four volumes rank among the best autobiographies ever written.

As for Sacheverell, an objective evaluation of his poetic oeuvre would have to acknowledge his extraordinary facility for mellifluous verse making, but would also have to admit that much of his verse reveals the prosodic displays of a technician rather the qualities of the supreme poet. More precisely, though his images were always highly effective, at times their cumulative effect was wanting.

There is no quarrel with the immense scale of his work; still, despite Pegasus always providing the proper rhythm, the Muses were not quite so generous with their inspiration. More to the point, Sacheverell's earliest poems, such as *The People's Palace* and *The Hundred and One Harlequins,* were fastidiously written and moderately successful. Certain poems of his middle period, such as *The Thirteenth Caesar* and *Cyder Feast,* reveal a virtuosity and further development. With his *Canons of Giant Art,* he produced a work of resonant splendor. John Smith overstated the case a bit when he recommended that Sacheverell's *Canons* was "a great inspiration, and must surely be seen, in the long run, as one of the finest poems of some length written in English in our time."[10]

It is primarily as a prose writer that Sacheverell will be remembered. His influence on the history of taste cannot be overemphasized. His interpretive lives of *Mozart, Liszt,* and *Scarlatti* are classics in their own right. His studies of art and architecture, especially *Southern Baroque Art, Conversation Pieces,* and *Narrative Pictures,* are contributions of the first order. To sum up or categorize Sacheverell's travel books is difficult. Unique in both subject matter and approach, they follow no formula and have no discernible pattern. For those who take to this literary genre, each is a delight, and among the best of the dozens of such guide books are *Spain, Arabesques and Honeycomb,* and *Bridge of the Brocard Sash.* "Surely no one else," Kenneth Clark once observed about Sacheverell, "had seen and heard so many beautiful things in so many places from Paris to Lagos";[11] and he could have added, no one else ever wrote about them so beautifully.

What the reputation of the Sitwells may be a decade or a century from now is difficult to forecast. The odds are that they will not be forgotten. Indications are that they are not destined for the oblivion they so often wished on their enemies. Similar to the Sitwells' own family revenant, who for hundreds of years was reputed to visit his living relatives to bestow an occasional kiss while they slept, Edith's poetry, Osbert's fiction and autobiographical volumes, and Sacheverell's art, music, and architectural tomes are destined to haunt the history of English literature for generations to come.

Notes and References

Preface

1. See "Dame Edith Sitwell, Poet, Dies; Stirred Literary Controversies," *New York Times*, 10 December 1964, 1, 41.

2. John W. Ehrstine, "Edith Sitwell: A Critical Bibliography, 1951–1973," *Bulletin of Bibliography* 31 (July–September 1974): 111–16.

3. As told to John Pearson, *Facades* (London: Macmillan, 1978), 107.

4. In a letter to Rache Lovat Dickson, 14 July 1949; *Letters to Macmillan,* ed. Simon Nowell-Smith (London: Macmillan, 1967).

Chapter One

1. Osbert Sitwell, *Left Hand, Right Hand* (London: Macmillan, 1945), 7; hereafter cited in the text as *LH.*

2. A limited edition (with an introduction by Osbert Sitwell) was published in London by the Dropmore Press, 1949.

3. Osbert Sitwell, *Laughter in the Next Room* (London: Macmillan, 1949), 134; hereafter cited in the text as *L.*

4. Edith Sitwell, *Taken Care Of* (London: Hutchinson, 1965), 15; hereafter cited in the text as *TC.*

5. Sacheverell Sitwell, *Splendours and Miseries* (London: Faber & Faber, 1943), 242–4.

6. Cf. Victoria Glendinning, *Edith Sitwell: A Unicorn among Lions* (New York: Knopf, 1981), 8–23; Pearson, *Facades,* 31–40; Geoffrey Elborn, *Edith Sitwell* (New York: Doubleday, 1981), 4–16; and Elizabeth Salter, *The Last Years of a Rebel* (Boston: Houghton Mifflin, 1967), 49–51.

7. As told to Pearson, *Facades,* 55.

8. In her *Notebook on William Shakespeare* (London: Macmillan, 1948), Edith asked, "Could the infinite variation and fertility of his genius be exhausted?" (228). Her commentaries on Shakespeare are filled with reverence, for she always approached the Bard with "a proper sense of humility" and in "awe of the subject" (1).

9. Salter, *The Last Years of a Rebel*, 21.

10. In her *Swinburne: A Selection* (London: Weidenfeld & Nicholson, 1960) she labeled him "one of the greatest poets England has produced . . . a supreme technician . . . a great tragic poet" (5).

11. Salter, *The Last Years of a Rebel*, 21.

12. Osbert Sitwell, *Great Morning* (London: Macmillan, 1947), 193.

13. *Great Morning*, 141.

14. As told to Pearson, *Facades*, 74.

15. Ibid., 99.

16. Osbert Sitwell, *Those Were the Days* (London: Macmillan, 1938), 4.

Chapter Two

1. Frank Swinnerton, *The Georgian Literary Scene* (London: Heinemann, 1935), 349.

2. Nina Harnett claims in her *Laughing Torso* (London: Constable, 1932), 87, that Nancy Cunard started *Wheels* and that "three young poets called Sitwell wrote for it."

3. *Wheels: Fourth Cycle* (Oxford: Blackwell, 1919), 14.

4. *Journals of Arnold Bennett: 1921–1928* (London: Cassell, 1933) 137.

5. In Edith's *Collected Poems* (London: Macmillan, 1961), giving a revised edition entitled "The Hambone and the Heart" (181–86).

6. "Some Notes on My Own Poetry," in ibid., xxxii.

7. *Poetry and Criticism* (London: Hogarth, 1925) 14.

8. Ibid., xxxiv.

9. R.L. Megroz, *The Three Sitwells* (London: Richards, 1927), 151.

10. Osbert wrote at length of his meeting with D'Annunzio in *Noble Essences: A Book of Characters* (London: Macmillan, 1950), 125–42.

11. Pearson, *Facades*, 129.

12. *Athenaeum*, 14 November 1919, 1208.

13. *Nation* (London) 26 (6 December 1919):352.

14. *Springfield Republican*, 29 February 1920, 9a.

15 *Who Killed Cock Robin?* (London: C. W. Daniel, 1921), 11; hereafter cited in the text as *W*.

Chapter Three

1. For a favorable reaction to the first public performance of *Facade* see Harold Acton's *Memoirs of an Aesthete* (London: Methuen, 1948), 128–9.

2. Coward later claimed that he did not walk out; but he did write a devastating spoof of the Sitwells, which he entitled *London Calling* (1923). In his play he depicted them as the Swiss Family Whittlebot—Hernia and her brothers Gob and Sago.

3. In his introduction to *Facade and Other Poems* (London: Duckworth, 1950), Jack Lindsay maintains that none of the poems in *Facade*, if carefully read, are nonsensical: "the associations are often glancing and rapid to the

extreme, but the total effect comes from a highly organized basis of sense" (18).

4. Some Notes on My Own Poetry," in *Collected Poems* (London: Duckworth, 1930), xxii; hereafter cited in the text as *CP*.

5. *Sunday Times* (London), 15 July 1926, 5.

6. Ibid.

7. Cecil Beaton, *The Wandering Years* (London: Weidenfeld & Nicholson, 1961), 234.

Chapter Four

1. *The Scarlet Tree* (London: Macmillan, 1946), 273.

2. Pearson, *Facades*, 127.

3. Introduction to *Collected Poems of Sacheverell Sitwell* (London: Duckworth, 1936), 15.

4. Preface to *Sacheverell Sitwell: Selected Poems* (London: Duckworth, 1942), vii.

5. Arnold Bennett, "Sitwells," *Adelphi* 7 (August 1923):316.

6. Edwin Muir, *Freeman* 7 (22 August 1923):571.

7. *New York Times*, 4 March 1923, 6.

8. John Smith, "Shall These Bones Live?" in *Sacheverell Sitwell: A Symposium*, ed. Derek Parker (London: Rota, 1975), 41.

9. Richard Aldington, *Literary Review*, 29 December 1923, 4.

10. Aldington, *Literary Review*, 9 June 1923, 747.

11. Aldington, *Life for Life's Sake* (New York: Viking, 1941), 203.

12. Aldington, "The Able Sitwells," *Saturday Review of Literature* 1 (2 August 1924):3.

13. Aldous Huxley, "The Tillotson Banquet," in *Mortal Coils* (London: Chatto & Windus, 1923), 149–50.

14. Ibid., 116.

15. "The Machine Breaks Down," in *Triple Fugue* (London: Richards, 1924), 186; hereafter cited in the text as *TF*.

16. Osbert Sitwell to Grant Richards, 17 November 1922; Humanities Research Center, University of Texas, Austin.

17. *New Statesman* 23 (2 August 1924):497.

18. Mary Ross, *New York Times Book Review*, 1 March 1925, 6.

19. F. H., *Nation and Athenaeum* 35 (19 July 1924):512.

20. Megroz, *The Three Sitwells*, 205.

21. Gerald Gould, *Saturday Review* 137 (28 June 1924): 670.

Chapter Five

1. C. M. Bowra, *Edith Sitwell* (Monaco: Lyrebird, 1947), 22.

2. In *Left Hand, Right Hand*, 89, Osbert refers to *The Sleeping Beauty*, labels Soldan's Song "lovely," and quotes from it at length.

3. Richard Le Gallienne, *New York Times Book Review*, 7 September 1924, 10.

4. Alan Porter, *Spectator* 132 (1924):599.

5. *Bookman* 60 (1924):227.

6. Babette Deutsch, *Liteary Review*, 23 August 1924, 980.

7. Cyril Connolly, *A Romantic Friendship* (London: Constable, 1975), 66.

8. Pearson, *Facades*, 190.

9. See Martin Green, *The Children of the Sun: A Narrative of "Decadence" in England After 1918* (New York: Basic Books, 1978), 78–80, 203–4, 216–17, 262–64, 360–66.

10. Ibid., 172.

11. As quoted by Pearson in *Facades*, 190.

12. Cyril Connolly, "Foi d'Estete," in *Sacheverell Sitwell: A Symposium*, ed. Parker, 6.

13. *Southern Baroque Art* (London: Richards, 1924), 9; hereafter cited in the text as *S*.

14. Megroz, *The Three Sitwells*, 288.

15. A. E. Coppard, *Saturday Review* 138 (1924):496.

16. *Discursions on Travel, Art and Life* (London: Richards, 1925), 5.

17. Ibid.

18. Bonamy Dobree, *Nation and Athenaeum* 37 (30 May 1935):271.

19. Easter 1925; in *Selected Letters of Edith Sitwell*, ed. John Lehmann and Derek Parker (London: Macmillan, 1970).

20. Louis Untermeyer, *Saturday Review of Literature* 2 (1925):367.

21. "Dead Fashion," *Times Literary Supplement*, 25 November 1926, 850.

22. Glendinning, *Edith Sitwell*, 115.

Chapter Six

1. *Before the Bombardment* (London: Duckworth, 1925), 66–67, hereafter cited in the text as *B*.

2. *Journals of Arnold Bennett*, 167.

3. John Lehmann, *A Nest of Tigers* (Boston: Little, Brown, 1968), 145.

4. As quoted by Roger Fulford, *Osbert Sitwell* (London: Longmans, Green, 1951), 21–22.

5. Ibid., 22.

6. *New York Times Book Review*, 14 November 1926, 7.

7. *All Summer in a Day* (London: Duckworth, 1926), ix.

8. Ibid., vii.

9. Ibid., x.

10. *Bookman* 64 (1927):748.

11. *Saturday Review of Literature* 3 (1926):593.

12. Kenneth Clark, " A Golden Pheasant," in *Sacheverell Sitwell: A Symposium*, ed. Parker, 17.

13. Rebecca West, *The Strange Necessity* (London: Jonathan Cape, 1928), 87.

14. Ibid., 88.

15. *All at Sea* (London: Duckworth, 1927), 94.

16. *England Reclaimed* (London: Duckworth, 1925), ii.

17. *New Statesman* 30 (1927):330.

18. *Nation* 125 (1927):382.

19. William York Tindall, *Forces in Modern British Literature* (New York, Knopf, 1947), 122.

20. *Selected Poems* (London: Duckworth, 1936), 47.

21. "Some Notes on My Own Poetry," in *Collected Poems*, xxxvi–xxxvii.

22. 11 July 1955; in *Selected Letters of Edith Sitwell,* ed. Lehmann and Parker, 199–200.

23. *Selected Poems*, 47.

24. "Some Notes on My Own Poetry," in *Collected Poems*, xii.

25. Kenneth Clark, "On the Development of Miss Sitwell's Later Style," *Horizon* 16 (1947):9

26. Undated letter to Wyndham Lewis, in *Letters of W. B. Yeats* (London Rupert Hart-Davis, 1954), 234.

Chapter Seven

1. *Alexander Pope* (London: Faber & Faber, 1930), 1; hereafter cited in text as *AP*.

2. Geoffrey Grigson, *Yorkshire Post*, 27 March 1930.

3. Mark Van Doren, *Books,* 13 April 1930, 5.

4. *Mozart* (London: Peter Davis, 1932), 99; hereafter cited in the text as *M*.

5. Ernest Newman, "An Amateur on Mozart," *Sunday Times* (London), 24 April 1932, 7.

6. "Mozart and Wagner," *Sunday Times* (London), 1 May 1932, 14.

7. Ernest Newman, "Mozart from All Points of View," *Sunday Times* (London), 15 May 1932, 5.

8. Ernest Newman, "More About Mr. Sacheverell Sitwell," *Sunday Times* (London), 22 May 1932, 7.

9. "Two Sitwells v. Newman," *Sunday Times,* (London), 29 May 1932, 7.

10. Introduction to *Collected Poems of Sacheverell Sitwell*, 23.

11. Lehmann, *A Nest of Tigers*, 167.

12. Letter dated June 1933; quoted by Elborn, *Edith Sitwell*, 107.

13. W. B. Yeats, *The Oxford Book of Modern Verse* (Oxford: Clarendon Press, 1936), xvii.

14. As told to Pearson, *Facades*, 293.

15. J. W. Alsop, *Books*, 18 March 1934, 14.

16. G. W. Stonier, *New Statesman and Nation* 6 (11 November 1933):605.

17. Elmer Davis, *Saturday Review of Literature* 10 (17 March 1934):554.

18. *New York Times*, 18 March 1934, 18.

19. Graham Greene, *Spectator* 151 (3 November 1933):638.

20. Ibid.

21. *Miracle on Sinai* (London: Duckworth, 1933), 87.

22. Ibid., 35.

23. Ibid., 17.

24. J. J. Reilly, *Commonweal* 25 (November 1936):54.

Chapter Eight

1. 8 May 1934; Humanities Research Center. Austin.

2. See Michael Holyroyd, *Lytton Strachey*, rev. ed. (London: Heinemann, 1973), 97.

3. 5 March 1936; Humanities Research Center.

4. Letter dated 20 August 1936; quoted by Pearson, *Facades*, 312.

5. John Sparrow, *Spectator* 156 (14 February 1936):262.

6. Elborn, *Edith Sitwell*, 122.

7. C. G. Stillman, *Books*, 2 August 1936, 3.

8. T. C. Mendenhall, *Saturday Review of Literature* 15 (14 November 1936):13.

9. The complete broadcast is found in W.B. Yeats, *Essays and Introductions* (London: Macmillan, 1961).

10. Letter dated 6 July 1935 in *Letters on Poetry from W. B. Yeats to Dorothy Wellesley* (London: Oxford University Press, 1940).

11. Letter dated 1934 May in John Sparrow's possession.

12. Introduction to *Collected Poems of Sacheverell Sitwell*, 26.

13. Ibid., 32.

14. Ibid., 27.

15. John Smith, "Shall These Bones Live?" in *Sacheverell Sitwell: A Symposium*, ed. Parker, 39.

16. See Parker Tyler, *The Divine Comedy of Pavel Tchelitchew* (New York: Fleet, 1967).

17. *I Live under a Black Sun* (London: Gollancz, 1937), 16.

18. Ibid., 116.

19. Ibid., 184.

20. Letter to David Horner, 3 October 1937; Humanities Research Center.

21. *Times Literary Supplement*, 2 October 1937, 713.

22. Evelyn Waugh, *Night and Day*, October 21, 1937, 7.

23. Empson to Edith Sitwell, April 1938; Humanities Research Center.

24. Letter to Raymond Marriott, February 1939; in *Selected Letters of Edith Sitwell*, ed. Lehmann and Parker.

25. Letter to E. M. Forster, 1 October 1939; Kings College Library, Cambridge.

26. Letter to John Lehmann, 15 June 1948; in *Selected Letters of Edith Sitwell*, ed. Lehmann and Parker.

27. Letter dated February 1937; Humanities Research Center.

28. Letter dated 5 May 1938; Humanities Research Center.

Chapter Nine

1. *Escape With Me!* (London: Macmillan, 1939), vii.

2. According to Pearson, *Facades*, 293.

3. Hamilton Fyfe, *Reynolds News*, 14 February 1940.

4. Ibid.

5. They were awarded £350 each plus costs, not an inconsiderable sum at the time if it be noted that Edith was paid £500 outright for her *Edith Sitwell's Anthology*, while *Look! The Sun* brought her only £100. See "The Suing Sitwell," *Time* 37 (3 March 1941):84.

6. *Sacred and Profane Love* (London: Faber & Faber, 1940), 40.

7. Ibid.

8. *Collected Poems of Edith Sitwell* (London, Macmillan, 1957), xli.

9. Ibid.

10. Ibid.

11. Bowra, *Edith Sitwell*, 35.

12. Mary Colum, review of *Street Songs, New York Times Book Review*, 23 May 1943, 22.

13. The text of Lehmann's broadcast can be found in *A Celebration for Edith Sitwell*, ed. José Garcia Villa (New York: New Directions, 1948), 78–82.

14. Elizabeth Drew, review of *Street Songs, Weekly Book Review*, 16 May 1943, 24.

15. Stephen Spender "Imagery in the Poetic World of Edith Sitwell," *A Celebration for Edith Sitwell*, 14.

16. Ibid., 16.

17. Undated letter quoted by Elborn, *Edith Sitwell*, 160–61.

18. Cited by Green, *Children of the Sun*, 362.

19. *A Nest of Tigers*, 189.

20. *Splendours and Miseries* (London: Faber & Faber, 1943), 242.

21. Letter dated 15 March 1945; Berg Collection, New York Public Library.

22. Letter dated 22 June 1945 to J. H. Hutchinson; Humanities Research Center.

23. Pearson, *Facades*, 382.

24. Letter dated 14 November 1944; Humanities Research Center.

25. Ibid.

26. *Poetry 1945–50* (London: Longmans, 1951), 63.

Chapter Ten

1. Clark, "On the Development of Miss Sitwell's Later Style,", 17.

2. L. P. Hartley "On *Left Hand, Right Hand,*" *Years Work in Literature*, 1949, 10.

3. *Spectator* 178 (21 March 1947):308.

4. *Times Literary Supplement*, 18 December 1948, 710.

5. Letter to Nancy Mitford, November 1948; in *The Letters of Evelyn Waugh* (London: Weidenfeld & Nicolson, 1980).

6. Osbert to Georgia Doble Sitwell, 13 February 1950; Humanities Research Center.

7. Ibid.

8. Letter dated 14 November 1948; in *The Letters of Evelyn Waugh*.

9. Ibid.

10. Harold Acton, *More Memories of An Aesthete* (London: Methuen, 1965), 178.

11. Letter to John Lehmann, February [?] 1945; Humanities Research Center.

12. Max Wykes-Joyce, *Triad of Genius* (London: Peter Owen, 1953), 117.

13. *Fanfare for Elizabeth* (London: Macmillan, 1946), 94.

14. Ibid., 31.

15. Ibid., 202.

16. Ibid., 1–2.

17. As quoted by Salter, *The Last Years of a Rebel*, 155.

18. Ibid.

19. T. S. Eliot to Edith, 11 June 1954; Humanities Research Center.

20. Compton Mackenzie, *Spectator,* 18 June 1954, 175.

21. "Some Notes on My Own Poetry," in *Collected Poems* (New York: Vanguard, 1954), xlix–l.

22. Salter, *The Last Years of a Rebel*, 148.

23. Ibid.

24. Ibid., 149.

25. Ibid.

26. Letter dated 14 July 1955: in *The Letters of Evelyn Waugh*.

27. Evelyn Waugh, *Sunday Times* (London), 7 December 1952.

28. Ibid.

29. Letter to Nancy Cunard, 8 March 1956; quoted by Pearson, *Facades*, 447.

30. G. Paulding, *New York Herald Book Review*, 6 September 1959, 4.

31. Edith Sitwell to Malcolm Bullock, 13 October 1959; Humanities Research Center.

32. Letter dated 26 September 1962; in *Selected Letters of Edith Sitwell*, ed. Lehmann and Parker.

33. Letter dated 3 October 1962; in ibid.

34. Lehmann, *A Nest of Tigers*, 274.

35. Michael Holyroyd, *Spectator*, 2 March 1962, 279.

36. Malcolm Muggeridge, *New Statesman* 63 (23 February 1963):267.

37. Letter to G.A. Cevasco, 9 May 1983; in his possession.

Chapter Eleven

1. F. R. Leavis, *New Bearings in English Poetry* (London: Chatto & Windus, 1932), 89.

2. Malcolm Muggeridge, *New Statesman* 63 (23 February 1962):267.

3. Geoffrey Grigson, *New York Review of Books* 4 (20 May 1965):11.

4. Evelyn Waugh, *Sunday Times* (London), 1 December 1952, 7.

5. Ibid.

6. Consult *Books in Print* (New York: Bowker, 1986–87), 3:4751. Prominent among more than a dozen of Edith's books will be found her *Poetry and Criticism, The Shadow of Cain, Gardeners and Astronomers, Alexander Pope,* and *I Live under a Black Sun.* Osbert is represented with more than twenty titles, mainly his fictional works, his autobiographical volumes, and a collection of his verse entitled *Selected Poems: Old and New.* Among Sacheverell's works readily available are his studies of *Mozart, Liszt, Scarlatti, Southern Baroque Art,* and several more of his art and architectural volumes, a few of his travel guides, and his *Collected Poems.*

7. Louise Bogan, *New York Times*, 10 December 1964, 41.

8. Cyril Connolly, *Sunday Times* (London), 29 July 1957, 14.

9. Allen Tate, *New York Times*, 10 December 1964, 41.

10. John Smith, "Shall These Bones Live?" *Sacheverell Sitwell: A Symposium*, ed. Parker, 46.

11. Kenneth Clark, "A Golden Pheasant," in ibid., 18.

Selected Bibliography

PRIMARY SOURCES

Edith Sitwell

1. Poetry
The Mother. Oxford: Blackwell, 1915.
Twentieth Century Harlequinade. Oxford: Blackwell, 1916. With Osbert.
Clowns' Houses. Oxford: Blackwell, 1918.
The Wooden Pegasus. Oxford: Blackwell, 1920.
Facade. London: Favil, 1922.
Bucolic Comedies. London: Duckworth. 1923.
The Sleeping Beauty. London: Duckworth, 1924.
Troy Park. London: Duckworth, 1925.
Elegy on Dead Fashion. London: Duckworth, 1926.
Rustic Elegies. London: Duckworth, 1927.
Gold Coast Customs. London: Duckworth, 1929.
Collected Poems. London: Duckworth, 1930.
Street Songs, London: Macmillan, 1942.
Green Songs and Other Poems, London: Macmillan, 1944.
Song of the Cold, London: Macmillan, 1945.
Canticle of the Rose, London: Macmillan, 1949.
Gardeners and Astronomers, London: Macmillan, 1953.
Collected Poems, London: Macmillan, 1954.

2. Fiction
I Live under a Black Sun. London: Gollancz, 1937.

3. Biography
Alexander Pope. London: Faber & Faber, 1930.
English Eccentrics. London: Faber & Faber, 1933.
Victoria of England. London: Faber & Faber, 1936.
Fanfare for Elizabeth. London: Macmillan, 1946.
The Queens and the Hive. London: Macmillan, 1962.

4. Social History
Bath. London: Faber & Faber, 1932.

5. Autobiography
Taken Care Of. London: Hutchinson, 1965.

6. Literary Criticism
Poetry and Criticism. London: Hogarth, 1925.
Pleasures of Poetry. London: Duckworth, 1932.
Aspects of Modern Poetry. London: Duckworth, 1934.

7. Anthologies
Wheels. First, second, third, fourth cycle. Oxford: Blackwell, 1916, 1917,
       1918, 1919. Fifth cycle. London: Leonard Parsons, 1920. Sixth cycle.
       London: C. W. Daniel, 1921.
Edith Sitwell's Anthology. London: Gollancz, 1940.
Poems Old and New. London: Gollancz, 1940.
Look! The Sun. London: Gollancz, 1941.
Atlantic Book of British and American Poetry. Boston: Little, Brown, 1958.

Osbert Sitwell

1. Poetry
Argonaut and Juggernaut. London: Chatto & Windus, 1919.
At the House of Mrs. Kinfoot. London: Favil, 1921.
Out of the Flame. London: Grant Richards, 1923.
England Reclaimed. London: Duckworth, 1927.
Selected Poems, Old & New. London: Duckworth, 1943.
Wrack at Tidesend: A Book of Balnearics. London: Macmillan, 1952.

2. Fiction
Triple Fugue. London: Grant Richards, 1924.
Before the Bombardment. London: Duckworth, 1926.
The Man Who Lost Himself. London: Duckworth, 1929.
Miracle on Sinai. London: Duckworth, 1933.
Those Were the Days. London: Macmillan, 1938.
Open the Door. London: Macmillan, 1941.

A Place of One's Own. London: Macmillan, 1941.
The Collected Stories of Osbert Sitwell. London: Duckworth, 1953.

3. Essays
Discursions on Travel, Art and Life. London: Grant Richards, 1925.
Penny Foolish. London: Macmillan, 1935.
Escape With Me! An Oriental Sketch Book. London: Macmillan, 1939.
Sing High! Sing Low!. London: Macmillan, 1944.
Pound Wise. London, Hutchinson, 1963.

4. Literary Criticism
Who Killed Cock Robin? London: C. W. Daniel, 1921.
Dickens. London: Chatto & Windus, 1932.

5. Drama
All at Sea. London: Duckworth, 1927. With Sacheverell.

6. Autobiography
Left Hand, Right Hand. London: Macmillan, 1945.
The Scarlet Tree. London: Macmillan, 1946.
Great Morning. London: Macmillan, 1948.
Laughter in the Next Room. London: Macmillan, 1949.
Noble Essences: A Book of Characters, London: Macmillan, 1950.

Sacheverell Sitwell

1. Poetry
The People's Palace. Oxford: Blackwell, 1918.
The Hundred and One Harlequins. London: Grant Richards, 1922.
The Thirteenth Caesar. London: Grant Richards, 1924.
Cyder Feast. London: Duckworth, 1927.
Canons of Giant Art. London: Faber and Faber, 1933.
Collected Poems. London: Duckworth, 1936.
Selected Poems. London: Duckworth, 1948.
An Indian Summer. London: Macmillan, 1982.

2. Cultural Studies
Southern Baroque Art. London: Grant Richards, 1924.
German Baroque Art. London: Duckworth, 1927.

Gothick North. London: Duckworth, 1929.
Spanish Baroque Art. London: Duckworth, 1931.
Mozart. London: Peter Davis, 1932.
Liszt. London: Faber & Faber, 1934.
Scarlatti. London: Faber & Faber, 1935.
Conversation Pieces. London: Batsford, 1936.
Narrative Pictures. London: Batsford, 1937.
Sacred and Profane Love. London: Faber & Faber, 1940.
Splendours and Miseries. London: Faber & Faber, 1943.
British Architecture and Craftsmen. London: Batsford, 1945.
The Hunters and Hunted. London: Macmillan, 1947.

3. Travel Guides
Mauretania. London: Duckworth, 1940.
The Netherlands. London: Batsford, 1948.
Spain. London: Batsford, 1950.
Portugal and Madeira. London: Batsford, 1954.
Denmark. London: Batsford, 1956.
Arabesque and Honeycomb. London: Robert Hale, 1957.
Bridge of the Brocard Sash. London: Weidenfeld & Nicholson, 1959.
Golden Wall and Mirador. London: Weidenfeld & Nicholson, 1961.

4. Autobiography
All Summer in a Day. London: Duckworth, 1926.
Dance of the Quick and the Dead. London: Faber & Faber, 1936.
Journey to the Ends of Time. London: Cassell, 1959.
For Want of a Golden City. London: Day, 1973.

5. Drama
All at Sea. London: Duckworth, 1927. With Osbert.

SECONDARY SOURCES

1. Bibliographies
Ehrstine, John W., and Rich, Douglas D., "Edith Sitwell: A Critical
    Bibliography, 1951–1973." *Bulletin of Bibliography* 31 (1974):111–
    16.

Elborn, Geoffrey. *Edith Sitwell*. New York: Doubleday, 1981. An appendix lists all of Edith's periodical contributions, translations, and musical settings (298–310).

Fifoot, Richard. *A Bibliography of Edith, Osbert and Sacheverell Sitwell*. London: Rupert Hart-Davis, 1963.

Rosenberg, Lois D. "Edith Sitwell: A Critical Bibliography, 1915–1950." *Bulletin of Bibliography* 21 (1953):40–43, 57–60.

2. Books and Articles

Bowra, C.M. *Edith Sitwell*. Monaco: Lyrebird, 1947. A brief, favorable study of her principal poems.

Brophy, James. *Edith Sitwell: The Symbolist Order*. Carbondale: University of Illinois Press, 1968. Discussion of Edith's place in the symbolist tradition.

Cevasco, G. A. "Edith Sitwell." In *Critical Survey of Poetry*, edited by F. M. Magill. New York: Salem, 1982, 6:2623–32. Analyzes her chief works and sums up her achievements.

Daiches, David. *Poetry and the Modern World*. 1940. Reprint. New York: Biblo & Tanner, 1969. The Sitwells as contemporary poets (61–89).

Deutsch, Babette. *This Modern World*. 1935. Reprint. New York: Norton, 1969. Evaluations of Edith's poetry (132–33, 165–66).

Elborn, Geoffrey. *Edith Sitwell*. New York: Doubleday, 1981. A biography that considers Edith's complexities, personal and creative, written with the cooperation of Sacheverell Sitwell.

Fraser, G. S. *The Modern Writer and His World*. New York: Praeger, 1964. Discussion of the Sitwells on 283–87 and passim.

Fulford, Roger. *Osbert Sitwell*. London: British Council, 1951. Brief biographical and critical study of its subject.

Fytton, Francis. "Edith Sitwell: Gothic Poet." *Catholic World* 183 (July 1956):292–98. Appraises Edith's poetry and focuses on her successful blending of the traditional and the ultramodern.

Glendinning, Victoria. *Edith Sitwell: A Unicorn among Lions*. New York: Knopf, 1981. A biography of its subject as a contemporary woman and gifted poet.

Jeremy, Sister M., O.P. "Clown and Canticle: The Achievement of Edith Sitwell." *Renascence* 3 (1951):128–37. An explication of *Gold Coast Customs, Street Song,* and *Canticle of the Rose.*

Lehmann, John. *A Nest of Tigers: The Sitwells in Their Time*. Boston: Little, Brown, 1968. An assessment of the trio and their works by one who knew them reasonably well.

Megroz, R. L. *The Three Sitwells*. London: Grant Richards, 1927. First critical study of the Sitwells.

Mills, Ralph J. *Edith Sitwell: A Critical Essay*. Grand Rapids, Mich.:

Eerdmans, 1966. A succinct study in Eerdman's *Contemporary Writers in Christian Perspective Series*.

Noon, William T., S.J. *Poetry and Prayer*. New Brunswick, N.J.: Rutgers University Press, 1967. Discussion of the anagogical aspects of Edith's religious verse (11–16).

Parker, Derek, ed. *Sacheverell Sitwell: A Symposium*. London: Rota, 1975. A series of nineteen mainly laudatory essays on the poetry, critical volumes, and travel books of its subject by such critics as Kenneth Clark, John Smith, Denys Sutton, Leonard Clark, and Cyril Connolly.

Pearson, John. *Facades: Edith, Osbert and Sacheverell Sitwell*. London: Macmillan, 1978. A comprehensive biography of the Sitwells—enhanced with over three dozen photographs—that portrays the trio as aesthetes, eccentrics, celebrities.

Pinto, Vivian de Sola. *Crisis in English Poetry, 1880–1940*. London: Hutchinson, 1967. Contends Edith's verse was the most important development in English poetry at the beginning of World War II (167–85).

Popkin, Henry. "Poets as Performers: The Revival of Poetry-Reading." *Theatre Arts* 36 (February 1952):27, 74. Discusses Edith's ability to deliver her lines of poetry.

Press, John. *A Map of Modern English Verse*. London: Oxford University Press, 1969. A consideration of Edith's contributions to and importance of *Wheels*.

Riding, Laura, and Graves, Robert. *A Survey of Modernist Poetry*. London: Heinemann, 1927. Discussion of the burlesque and humorous elements in Edith's early poetry (230–35, 247–49).

Salters, Elizabeth. *The Last Years of a Rebel: A Memoir of Edith Sitwell*. Boston: Houghton Mifflin, 1967. A personal account of Edith's last years by the woman who was her secretary and confidante.

Villa, Jose Garcia, ed. *A Celebration for Edith Sitwell*. New York: New Directions, 1948. Contains appreciative essays by such poets and critics as Gordon Bottomly, Kenneth Clark, Horace Gregory, John Lehmann, Stephen Spender, Gertrude Stein, and W. B. Yeats.

Wykes-Joyce, Max. *Triad of Genius*. London: Owen, 1953. A biography that focuses on the public life and literary accomplishments of the three Sitwells.

Index